ESSENTIALS
of
HEALTH AND SAFETY
AT WORK

HSE
Health & Safety
Executive

LONDON: HMSO

Applications for reproduction should be made to HMSO.
Any enquiries about this publication should be addressed to the
Health and Safety Executive at any area office or at one of the
public enquiry points:

Health and Safety Executive
Library and Information Services
Broad Lane
SHEFFIELD S3 7HQ
Telephone: 0742 752539 Telex: 54556

Health and Safety Executive
Library and Information Services
Baynards House
1 Chepstow Place
Westbourne Grove
LONDON W2 4TF
Telephone: 071 221 0870 Telex: 25683

ISBN 0 11 885445 3

FOREWORD

Over 500 people die each year at work and several hundred thousand lose time through injury or illness.

Quite apart from the suffering of the workers and their families the cost to business is huge. For employers, controlling accidents and ill health means less compensation to pay, lower repair bills and less lost production. It is profitable to reduce accidents, damage and the minor fires which can so easily turn into major losses.

Workplace accidents can be prevented - and you don't have to turn your place upside down or spend a lot of money to do so. You only need to use good business sense and to follow well-recognised principles.

But you need a commitment to do things properly, so that safety becomes as much part of every job as production, quality or cost. Like everything else in business, safety does not just happen - you have to **make** it happen.

As your business grows you will be less able to know every detail of what goes on. That is why it makes sense to get employees involved with health and safety right from the very beginning, so they will not tolerate hazards and unsafe practices which can cause accidents or damage.

I commend this booklet to all at work, especially to those running small firms or with limited business experience - but everyone can be sure of finding something in it which will help them recognise and deal with health and safety problems at work.

Its message is simple: safe and healthy working practices are good working practices. Everyone stands to benefit by following this commonsense safety code.

C M Thomas

Health and Safety Commission

CONTENTS

About this book

This book illustrates the general scope of the laws covering health and safety at work and following it will help you comply with the law. It will be of particular value to anyone starting up a new firm, managing a small work unit or preparing a safety policy for a company.

Whatever kind of business you run there will be risks to health and safety. The first step towards controlling those risks is to recognise them.

This book helps by giving practical guidance on how to identify work hazards, assess the risks to employees and others and plan the actions needed to reduce or eliminate risk. It will not make you an expert in occupational health and safety but it will help you decide whether you need further information or specialist assistance.

It does not give definitive legal advice for all situations: references to particular laws are there as examples of general points. There may be other standards required by specific legislation applying in your particular business.

HOW TO USE THIS BOOK

Sections 1-5 are relevant to everyone and suggest ways of organising, and things to find out, to improve management of health and safety in your business.

Sections 6-19 identify particular hazards and necessary precautions. Look at relevant parts once you have thought about your work and the risks it involves. Not all the hazards described will apply to your business. Most chapters tell you about some of the laws which might apply to you, and about useful Health and Safety Executive (HSE) publications.

The reference section is a guide to sources of further information, including a list of HSE publications mentioned in the text by their reference number (eg AS 11) are described more fully in the publications list, together with a small selection of other guidance material.

WHERE TO GET FURTHER HELP

Although in many cases you don't have to be an expert to see that something is dangerous or to know how to put it right, the solution to a safety problem sometimes requires detailed knowledge and experience. Your local health and safety inspector can help you get proper advice.

Offices, shops, warehouses, restaurants, hotels etc should consult their local authority inspector, usually in the Council's Environmental Health Department. For the address of the nearest inspector look in the phone book.

HSE inspectors deal with most other businesses. They can be contacted at the offices listed at the back of this book.

Advice on health at work and first aid can be obtained from the Employment Medical Advisory Service - contact your local HSE office for information.

Small firms can benefit from using professional health and safety services, occasionally or regularly. There are various independent consultancies, safety groups and schemes, or you may be able to use the services of a larger firm you work for. Your health and safety inspector can help you find suitable advice. Some other useful addresses are listed at the back of this book.

ACKNOWLEDGEMENTS

Some of the placards and illustrations shown in this book are reproduced by courtesy of the British Safety Council and the Royal Society for the Prevention of Accidents.

NOTE

Some subjects, such as civil claims for accident compensation, are specialist areas in their own right. They are not covered in this book and are not dealt with by your local health and safety inspector.

To start organising for safety you need to know about the occupational safety laws which affect you. Here is a guide to some basic legal requirements and how the law is administered.

THE MAIN LAWS

Health and Safety at Work etc Act 1974 (HSW Act)

The HSW Act requires you to ensure, so far as is reasonably practicable, the health and safety of yourself and others who may be affected by what you do or fail to do.

You have duties towards people who:

- work for you, including casual workers, part-timers, trainees and subcontractors

- use workplaces you provide (if you are a landlord, for example)

- are allowed to use your equipment

- visit your premises (customers or contractors)

- may be affected by your work (your neighbours, the public and other work people)

- use products you make, supply or import

- use your professional services (if you are, say, a designer).

The HSW Act applies to all work premises and activities, and everyone at work - employee, supervisor, manager, director or self-employed - has responsibilities under the Act.

Other laws

In addition there are specific laws applying to certain premises. The main ones are:

- the Factories Act 1961

- the Offices, Shops and Railway Premises Act 1963.

Other specific acts apply to activities such as agriculture and quarrying. There are also regulations made under these acts which set standards for cleanliness, machinery safety and so on.

The range of workplaces covered by these laws is wider than their names suggest. Some places which are not obviously 'factories' - like scrapyards, building sites and abattoirs - come under the Factories Act, for example. In this book, shorthand phrases like 'industrial firms' or 'farms' mean all the premises covered by the relevant act.

MEETING THE LEGAL STANDARDS

Some acts or regulations are specific - setting out, for instance, how a certain job should be done or how a particular machine should be guarded.

Nowadays, these details are usually published in codes of practice approved under the HSW Act. Although you do not have to follow them exactly, you do have to meet their standards in an equally satisfactory way.

Often, however, laws are expressed in fairly general terms and, over the years, the Courts have decided what has to be done. Safe practices in one industry are often used as the standard in another. For example, the way in which ladders are required by law to be secured against slipping in the building trades is a good guide to the safety precautions necessary wherever ladders are used.

A few laws require you to do things irrespective of the cost or time involved. Generally, though, you have to do what is 'reasonably practicable' - and inspectors are guided by that when they give you advice. If you disagree with the advice, discuss the issue with your inspector or, if you cannot resolve the matter, with his or her boss.

There is a list of further guidance material at the back of the book.

DID YOU KNOW THAT BY LAW ...

- commercial and industrial firms must notify their inspector that they are running their business?

- you must display certain documents, for example an approved poster (or individual leaflets) to comply with the Health and Safety Information for Employees Regulations and an Employers' Liability (Compulsory Insurance) Certificate?

- children (under 16 years old) are generally prohibited from working in industrial activities and there are also restrictions on the part-time employment of children in other jobs?

- certain categories of accidents, occupational diseases and dangerous occurrences must be reported? See section 5, *Accidents and emergencies.*

- some processes - melting lead scrap, for instance - may not be operated by women or young people, and some machines may only be used by them under proper supervision?

- people employed on hazardous processes may have to be medically examined by a doctor or nurse from the Employment Medical Advisory Service (EMAS)?

- some jobs require specified protective clothing or equipment, or specified standards of health?

- safety representatives - appointed by a recognised trade union - must be allowed to investigate accidents and potential hazards, pursue employees complaints and carry out inspections of the workplace? They are entitled to certain information and to paid time off to train for their health and safety role.

- you may need to train and appoint someone to carry out certain tasks such as inspecting power press guards or mounting abrasive wheels?

- you may need an outside expert - such as an insurance company engineering surveyor - to carry out periodic tests and examinations of equipment such as boilers, lifts or cranes?

- you cannot 'delegate' the legal responsibility for ensuring that employees follow safe working practices and you may need to vet the methods used by contractors working for you?

See: Leaflet, Health and Safety Law

ENFORCING THE LAW

Health and safety laws relating to your firm will be enforced by an inspector either from HSE (eg a factory inspector or an agricultural inspector) or from your local council (usually an environmental health officer).

Inspectors may visit workplaces without notice but you are entitled to see their identification before they come in. They may want to investigate an accident or complaint, or examine the safety, health and welfare aspects of your business.

They have the right to talk to employees and safety representatives, take photographs and samples and even, in certain cases, to impound dangerous equipment. They are entitled to cooperation and answers to questions.

Inspectors are aware of the special needs of small firms and will give you help and advice on how to comply with the law.

If there is a problem they may issue a formal notice requiring improvements or, where serious danger exists, one which prohibits the use of a process or equipment. If you receive an Improvement or Prohibition Notice you may appeal to an Industrial Tribunal.

Inspectors have powers to prosecute a firm (or an individual) for breaking health and safety law.

WHERE TO FIND OUT MORE ABOUT THE LAW

HSE publications can help explain legal requirements but for full details of a particular law you will need to refer to the act or regulation itself (through booksellers, HMSO or your local library).

Your inspector can help you find out more about relevant laws - some of which may apply to you even though they are not mentioned in this book.

Keeping a business safe is a continuing exercise. Begin by deciding what you want to achieve. Follow these 11 steps to review the risks and safeguards in your operations, and where you might benefit from a 'safety improvement plan'.

KNOW YOUR LEGAL DUTIES

If you have people working for you, or are a supplier of goods or services, there are laws protecting those whom you might affect. Find out about the occupational safety laws which apply to you.

PROVIDE SAFE METHODS

Find out about safe working methods for your industry and see what published guidance is available. Make sure everyone is aware of the correct procedures - consider displaying warning notices in workplaces or near machines, or preparing simple checklists of local rules.

ORGANISE THE DUTIES

You probably have to work through your managers, supervisors and employees. Decide who is responsible for which safety duties, making sure that there are no overlaps or gaps, and that everyone knows their own responsibilities.

Here are some suggestions for a supervisor's duties...

Ensure, for your section, that:

- you are familiar with the company safety policy and your section's 'arrangements'

- employees are trained and aware of the hazards at their workplace

- staff know where to find first aid and fire fighting equipment

- supervision is available at all times, particularly for young or inexperienced workers

- safety rules are observed and, for example, protective equipment is worn or used

- safety devices are properly adjusted and maintained

- machinery and equipment is frequently inspected to make sure it is properly maintained and safe to use

- any defects are promptly reported and rectified

- good standards of housekeeping are maintained

- you regularly review working practices to improve health and safety

- you investigate accidents and incidents, and recommend ways of preventing recurrences.

PREPARE A SAFETY POLICY

If you have five or more employees you must have a written safety policy which sets out the organisation (people and responsibilities) and arrangements (systems and procedures) for carrying it out. Bring it and any revision to the attention of your employees.

Make clear your commitment to high standards of health and safety. Sign and date the policy and remember to review it periodically.

The references on these pages are described more fully in the publications list at the back of the book.

HSC
Health & Safety
Commission

Writing a safety
policy statement

Advice to
employers

TRAIN YOUR STAFF

Give employees information and training so they know and understand the arrangements for handling particular hazards.

Sometimes formal training in health and safety will be necessary. Start with supervisors who have responsibility for work methods and job instruction. Use safety checklists as a guide in training.

Specific training requirements apply to some activities, for example young people using certain machines. Remember that proper training and supervision is particularly important for all young people because they may not recognise dangers. Show them HSE leaflet IND(G)2(L).

TRAIN YOURSELF

When you walk around your premises look for things which are unsafe or potentially unsafe. Learn to identify hazards and the ways of dealing with them. Take the advice of your employees, insurance company, local inspector and, for health problems, the Employment Medical Advisory Service. Keep up to date - with information from, for example:

- the Health and Safety Commission (HSC). Its bi-monthly 'Newsletter' reviews HSE publications, changes in safety law and similar items of interest

- safety organisations like the Royal Society for the Prevention of Accidents (RoSPA) and the British Safety Council (BSC). They also provide training courses

- monthly safety magazines like *Health and Safety at Work, Occupational Safety and Health* (RoSPA) and *Safety Management* (BSC)

- employers' organisations and trade unions which provide guidance on safety aspects of their industry. Seek more specialist advice if you need it.

CHECK YOUR PERFORMANCE

Having set the standards for your firm, check that the rules are being followed and monitor how well you are doing.

Inspections can be informal, say by a supervisor at the beginning of the working day, or formal - say once a quarter. Use checklists or notes to make sure you don't miss important points.

Look for information which will help you evaluate hazards and make improvements. Don't forget to check for the expected improvements at the next inspection.

ORGANISE YOUR INFORMATION

Keep your safety documentation separately organised and filed. Don't let information - like letters from your local inspector, insurance company reports, and safety and health information from suppliers - go astray. Use it to check that you are operating to the highest standards and that your safety policy is up to date.

INVESTIGATE WHEN THINGS GO WRONG

Investigation of accidents, dangerous occurrences and 'near misses' helps prevent recurrences. Don't investigate to attribute blame; concentrate on analysing the facts so you can make sensible decisions about remedial action. Incidents rarely have a single cause - usually they result from a combination of actions, errors or failures of people and equipment.

PREPARE YOUR 'SAFETY IMPROVEMENT PLAN'

If you find that changes are needed, decide on your priorities and how they are going to be dealt with. This plan might help you organise the work.

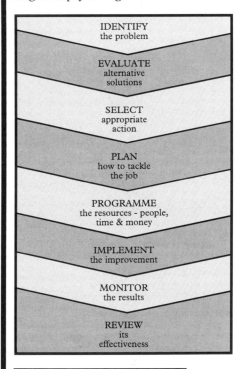

IDENTIFY
the problem

EVALUATE
alternative
solutions

SELECT
appropriate
action

PLAN
how to tackle
the job

PROGRAMME
the resources - people,
time & money

IMPLEMENT
the improvement

MONITOR
the results

REVIEW
its
effectiveness

MAINTAIN INTEREST

You need the cooperation and active commitment of supervisors and all employees. Draw on their ideas and experience through regular health and safety meetings and briefings. If safety representatives have been appointed by trade unions you recognise, you must consult them. Encourage employees by regular review of safety reports and staff suggestions. Use posters, safety committees, and displays of safety performance.

It is the duty of every employer ...

'... to provide systems of work that are, so far as is reasonably practicable, safe and without risks to health'
(Health and Safety at Work etc Act, Section 2)

Successful organisation does not come about by chance, but as a result of a system. To get work done safely you need a 'safe system of work'. Safety is part of management.

The references on these pages are described more fully in the publications list at the back of the book.

A SAFE AND HEALTHY SYSTEM OF WORK

'Health' and 'safety' are not always separate issues - correct use of protective clothing and equipment, for example, may deal with both. To develop a safe system think of both aspects, whether dealing with people, animals, machines or substances.

Health ...

- would a worker know what might happen to his or her overalls or skin if they were splashed with chemicals?

- could poor design of working areas, poor posture or repetitive movements lead to pain and soreness - in a keyboard operator's arms, for instance?

- is there any risk of animals transmitting diseases?

- what is the likely level of exposure when using a toxic solvent to clean a machine? Can exposure be reduced by substitution or alterations to the process?

Safety ...

- would an electrician working near a roof covered in fragile materials know of the danger unless told about it?

- what control methods or standard of housing would be required for the safety of an animal, its handler and the public bearing in mind its behaviour and temperament?

- would there be any hazard if a machine or its guard failed, or if the operator chose to do the job a different way?

- are staff vulnerable to physical violence from robbers, hooligans or the people they deal with?

- is there any fire hazard from the use and storage of a cleaning chemical, or from disposal of contaminated cloths?

Health risks may be less obvious than safety hazards but are just as important. Once you have identified the risks, a safe system will provide adequate protection against them - and workers should be encouraged to keep to it.
See: IND(G)76(L)

PERMITS TO WORK

Simple instructions may be adequate for most jobs, but some - particularly where the ordinary routine of production work is broken - require an extra level of care. Maintenance activities or occasional working in confined spaces are examples. Issuing a safe written procedure is a good discipline but when the possible risks are very great a formal permit system may be needed.

A 'permit to work' states exactly what work is to be done and when, and which parts are safe. A responsible person should assess the work and check safety at each stage. The people doing the job sign the permit to show that they understand the hazards and precautions necessary.
See: GN:GS 5

PERMIT-TO-WORK CERTIFICATE

PLANT DETAILS (Location identifying number, etc.)		
WORK TO BE DONE	The above plant has been removed from service and ... under my supervision have been informed	ACCEPTANCE OF CERTIFICATE

PEOPLE

Don't forget the needs of the individuals doing the job - for instance:

- protective gear, seating, working space and machinery guarding which is suitable for each individual

- ability to work safely if they are affected by medicines, drugs or alcohol, or have recently suffered illness or injury

- ability to understand safety instructions, through differences of language or culture

- appropriate methods, facilities or emergency procedures for those who have partial sight, poor hearing or some other handicap eg epilepsy.

- you may need to make special provision for the health and safety of persons working alone.

See: IND(G)73(L)

MAINTENANCE

It's not only organisation of the work which makes a safe system - it's also the condition of the equipment, buildings or plant used. All need to be properly maintained.

Systems for maintenance range from daily inspections carried out by an operator through to full tests and examinations by a competent person such as an engineering surveyor from an insurance company.

It is good practice to get the person carrying out any check or maintenance to confirm the checks performed and to record the defects remedied. A record card hanging on a machine is useful for daily checks, and a log book for more detailed weekly inspections. A written record should be kept following each visual inspection, thorough examination or major repair or modification of the plant. Some thorough examinations and tests are required by law and in these cases there is usually a requirement for the details to be recorded in a register.

MONITORING THE SYSTEM

You cannot rely on your systems always being right. Review them periodically to ensure that changes in staff, materials, equipment, location or timing do not introduce new hazards.

Check the system works by seeing that the rules and precautions not only deal adequately with all the risks but are also being followed by those doing the work - particularly if they are working outside 'normal hours' with less supervision than usual.

Inspections are more effective if done systematically and regularly. Record the results so that progress or deterioration in standards can be assessed. The information you collect should provide you with knowledge about levels of supervision, adequacy of training and the systems of work actually being followed. Does your safety policy reflect what is happening in practice?

Organise safety in the same way as you organise your other sysyems. Delegate responsibility only to capable people. Get a report back about any unexpected hazards encountered so that next time you can plan to deal with them.

CHECKLIST

Ask youself some questions about the jobs - regular, irregular and the 'one-offs' - in your firm:

- who is in charge of the job?

- do their responsibilities over-lap with those of anyone else?

- is there anything which is not someone's responsibility?

- are there any established safe ways of doing the job?

- are there any relevant codes of practice or guidance notes?

- are there safe working procedures laid down for the job?

- can the job be made safe so protective clothing is not needed?

- have people been instructed in the use and limitations of protective clothing?

- has anyone assessed whether equipment, tools or machines have the capacity for the job?

- what will be the consequences if you are wrong?

- how will the person in charge deal with any problems?

- if things do go wrong, would your people know what to do? Could emergency services get to the site?

- if the job cannot be finished today can it be left in a safe state? Are clear instructions available for the next shift?

- are your production people aware of what maintenance staff are doing, and vice versa?

- is there a system for checking that jobs are done safely in the way intended?

4 PROTECTIVE CLOTHING AND EQUIPMENT

Before resorting to protective clothing and equipment remember you have a duty to eliminate or control the risk, as far as is reasonably practicable, by some other means.

CHOOSING AND USING EQUIPMENT

Provide the right grade of protection, appropriate to the risk. Many jobs require, by law, specified clothing or 'approved' equipment. Explain clearly the requirements of the job to your supplier and get specialist advice where necessary.

Choose good quality products made to a recognised or approved standard.

Choose equipment which is suitable for the person using it - consider size, fit and weight. Let the users help choose it - they will then be more likely to cooperate in using it.

Equipment must be compatible with other items and be a correct fit - for example a respirator may not give proper protection if air leaks around the faceseal because the user has a beard or is wearing spectacles.

Make sure the user knows why the item is needed, when it has to be used and what its limitations are. Instruct, train and supervise in its use.

In high risk situations, the use of protective clothing and equipment is essential. Check regularly and investigate any reasons for non-use. Don't allow exemptions for jobs which take 'just a few minutes'. Safety signs are useful reminders.

Don't forget that visitors and workers nearby, as well as those directly employed in a hazard area, may need to be provided with the appropriate protection.

Equipment needs to be well looked after and stored in a dry, uncontaminated room, cupboard or box. Keep it clean and in good repair. Make sure replacements are readily available.

By law, necessary equipment must be provided free. Employees must make full and proper use of it, take reasonable care of it and report its loss, destruction or any defect.

EYES

Hazards: chemical or metal splash; dust; projectiles; gas and vapour; radiation.

Choices: spectacles; goggles; face screens; helmets.

Note: some processes require the use of eye protection made to an approved specification - most equipment is marked with the appropriate British Standard number. Impact protection ranges from highest standard (grade 1) to 'basic' use. Various combinations of dust (D), gas (G), molten metal (M) and liquid splash protection are available.

HEAD AND NECK

Hazards: impact from falling or flying objects; risk of head bumping; hair entanglement; chemical drips or splash; adverse climate or temperature. Risk of contaminating products by hair contact

Choices: helmets; bump caps; hairnets; hats; caps; beard snoods; sou'westers and cape hoods; skull-caps.

Note: some safety helmets incorporate or can be fitted with specially designed respiratory or hearing protection. Don't forget neck protection eg scarves for use during welding.

There is a list of further guidance material at the back of the book.

HEARING

Hazards: impact noise; high intensities (even if short exposure); pitch (high and low frequency).

Choices: earplugs or muffs.

Note: earplugs may be pre-shaped or individually moulded in rubber or plastic, or disposable - made of compressible plastic foam, glass-down etc. Can be joined by coloured cord for use in food preparation. Take advice to make sure they can reduce ('attenuate') noise to an acceptable level. Fit only specially designed ear muffs over safety helmets.

HANDS AND ARMS

Hazards: abrasion; temperature extremes; cuts and punctures; impact; chemicals; electric shock; skin infection, disease or contamination; vibration. Risk of product contamination.

Choices: gloves; gauntlets; mitts; wrist cuffs; armlets.

Note: don't wear gloves or mitts when operating machines such as bench drills where the gloves might get caught. Some materials are quickly penetrated by chemicals - care in selection is needed. Use skin conditioning cream after work with water or fat solvents. Barrier creams provide limited protection against infection etc. Disposable or cotton inner gloves can reduce sweating.

FEET AND LEGS

Hazards: wet; electrostatic build-up; slipping; cuts and punctures; falling objects; heavy pressures; metal and chemical splash; abrasion.

Choices: safety boots and shoes with steel toe caps (and steel mid-sole); gaiters; leggings; spats and clogs.

Note: footwear can have a variety of sole patterns and materials to prevent slips in different conditions, have oil or chemical-resistant soles, and be anti-static, electrically conductive or insulating. There is a variety of styles including 'trainers' and ankle supports. Avoid high heeled shoes and open sandals.

RESPIRATORY PROTECTION

Hazards: toxic and harmful dusts; gases and vapours; harmful micro organisms such as bacteria and viruses.

Choices: disposable respirators; half masks or full face mask respirators fitted with filtering cartridge or canister; powered respirators blowing filtered air to a mask, visor, helmet, hood or blouse; fresh air hose equipment; breathing apparatus (self contained and fresh air line types).

Note: the right type of respirator filter must be used as each is effective for only a limited range of substances. Cartridges and canisters have only a limited life. Where there is a shortage of oxygen or any danger of losing consciousness from fumes etc, use only breathing apparatus - **never use a filtering cartridge**. All equipment should be suitable for its purpose and should meet the approval requirements of HSE - if in doubt ask the manufacturer/supplier.

A chain saw operator might need all this equipment...

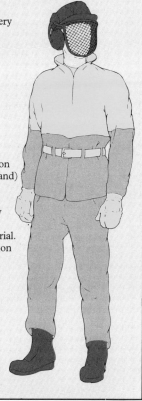

safety helmet
(replace at intervals recommended by the manufacturer - eg every 2-3 years)

ear defenders

eye protection

clothing
(should be close fitting)

gloves
(with protective pad on the back of the left hand)

protection for legs
(incorporating loosely woven long nylon fibres or similar material. All round leg protection is recommended).

chain saw operator boots
(the casual user may obtain adequate protection by a combination of protective spats and industrial steel toe-capped safety boots)

PROTECTING THE BODY

Hazards: heat; cold; bad weather; chemical or metal splash; spray from pressure leaks or spray guns; impact or penetration; contaminated dust; excessive wear or entanglement of own clothing. Risk of contaminating product or food.

Choices: conventional or disposable overalls; boiler suits; warehouse coats; donkey jackets; aprons and specialist protective clothing.

Note: materials choice includes: non-flammable; anti-static; chainmail; chemically impermeable; high visibility. Don't forget other protection, like safety harnesses or lifejackets.

See: AI 1

EMERGENCY EQUIPMENT

Careful selection, maintenance and regular operator training is needed for equipment like compressed air escape breathing apparatus, artificial respirators and safety ropes or harnesses.

5 ACCIDENTS AND EMERGENCIES

You need to respond quickly in an emergency, whether it's a simple accident or a major incident. Plan how to deal with possible problems. Some need to be reported to your inspector.

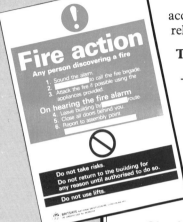

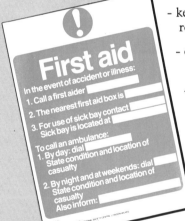

CONTROLLING AN INCIDENT

Plan for reasonably foreseeable incidents. You may need a written emergency plan if a major incident at your works might involve risks to the public, rescuing employees, or coordination of the emergency services.

Plan for what might go wrong ...

accidents? explosion? flood? poisoning? electrocution? fire? release of radioactivity? broken bones? chemical spill?

Tell people:

- what might happen and how the alarm will be raised

- what to do, including how to call the emergency services

- where to go to reach safety or get rescue equipment

- who will control the incident, and the names of other key people such as the first aiders

- essential actions such as emergency plant shut down or making processes safe.

Checklist

- keep any access ways for emergency services and all escape routes clear

- clearly label important items like shut off valves, electrical isolators and fire fighting equipment

- make sure emergency plans cover night and shift working, weekends and (possibly) times when the premises are closed eg holidays

- train everyone in emergency procedures, eg fire drills, and don't forget the special needs of disabled people

- test emergency equipment regularly - disposable eyewash bottles should not have been opened and used, for example

- assist the emergency services by clearly marking your premises from the road. Consider drawing up a simple plan marked with the location of hazardous items

- have a system to account for staff and visitors in the event of an evacuation

AFTER AN ACCIDENT OR SERIOUS INCIDENT

- treat any injuries and deal with the immediate emergency

- make the premises safe

- if applicable, report the details to your inspector

- record any injuries in your accident book

- as far as possible during rescue, clearing up operations or your own investigations, take care not to destroy the evidence which your inspector might require during investigation of the circumstances. If in doubt, check with the inspector.

The references on these pages are described more fully in the publications list at the back of the book.

FIRST AID

Immediate and proper examination and treatment of injuries may save life - and is essential to reduce pain and help injured people make a quick recovery. Neglect or inefficient treatment of an apparently trivial injury may lead to infection and ill health. All businesses must have an appropriate level of first aid treatment available Health and Safety (First Aid) Regulations 1981.

For most small firms ...

Appoint someone to take charge in an emergency, to call an ambulance, and to look after the first aid equipment. At least one 'appointed person' must be available at all times when people are at work.

Provide - and keep clean - a first aid box containing only first aid material. The box should contain guidance on the treatment of injured people - in particular how to keep someone alive by artificial respiration, how to control bleeding and how to deal with an unconscious patient. Keep the box near washing facilities.

Display - notices giving the locations of first aid equipment and the name and location of the appointed person or first aider.

In some cases, where there are special hazards, you may need a first aid room, a qualified first aider or someone with specialist first aid training.

As your company grows, reassess your need for qualified first aiders. First aiders must have training appropriate to the hazards of the workplace. A trained first aider issued with a certificate which is valid for three years only - after that a refresher course and re-examination is necessary. Organisations carrying out the training of first aiders must be registered through EMAS - ask your local Employment Medical Adviser.

In all firms it makes sense to have someone who knows the basics of first aid eg resuscitation, control of bleeding, and treatment of an unconscious patient.

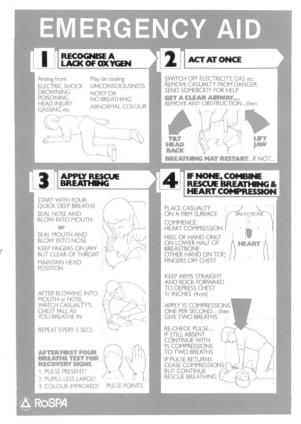

See: IND(G)3(L)

Health and Safety (First Aid) Regulations 1981
See: HS(R)11 (Guidance Booklet and Approved Code of Practice)

REPORTING ACCIDENTS AND DISEASE

All injuries should be recorded in the accident book. Some injuries, diseases and dangerous occurrences must also be reported to your inspector.

Reporting of Injuries, Diseases and Dangerous Occurrences Regulations 1985 applying to all employers and the self-employed, and covering everyone at work, require you to:

report immediately by phone if as a result of (or in connection with) your work ...

- someone dies, receives a major injury, or is seriously affected by, for example, electric shock or poisoning

- there is a 'dangerous occurrence' ('near miss').

See: HSE 11

send a written report to ...

- confirm, within seven days, a telephone report of a death, major injury or dangerous occurrence

- notify, within seven days of the accident, any injury which stops someone doing their normal job for more than three days

- report certain diseases suffered by workers who do specified types of work (See: HSE 17)

- report certain events involving flammable gas in domestic and other premises.

Have copies of the report form (F2508) ready for use. See: HS(R)23

6 GENERAL WORKING ENVIRONMENT

Use these seven checklists to find out what facilities you may need to make the workplace safe and healthy and to provide a reasonable standard of welfare for workers and visitors alike.

HYGIENE AND WELFARE

- separate toilets for each sex (subject to certain exemptions), marked appropriately

- toilets ventilated, kept clean, in working order and easily accessible

- ventilated space between toilet and any workroom

- wash basin with hot and cold (or warm) running water

- soap and towels (or electric hand dryer). Nail brush where required

- barrier cream, skin cleansers and skin conditioning cream provided where necessary

- waste bins (regularly emptied)

- special hygiene precautions where necessary (eg showers, or long handled ta where food is handled)

- adequate provision for workers away from base

- drying space for wet clothes

- lockers or hanging space for work/home clothing

- clean drinking water supply - clearly marked

- adequate facilities for taking food and drink, particularly for shift and night-time workers, with wash-up sink and means of heating water.

CLEANLINESS

- premises, furniture and fittings kept clean

- good housekeeping to clear trade waste, dirt and refuse regularly

- rubbish and food waste covered and regularly removed to keep premises clear of pests

- regular cleaning up of spillages

- floors and steps washed or swept regularly

- internal walls and ceilings washed or painted regularly

FLOORS AND GANGWAYS

- kept clean, dry and not slippery

- good drainage in wet processes

- suitable footwear or working platforms provided where necessary

- ramps kept dry and with non-skid surfaces

- gangways and roadways well marked and kept clear

- level, even surfaces without holes or broken boards

- floor load capacities posted in lofts, storage areas etc

- salting/sanding and sweeping of outdoor routes during icy or frosty conditions

- steps, corners and fixed obstacles clearly marked eg by black and yellow diagonal stripes

- floor openings, eg vehicle examination pits, kept covered when not in use and the edges clearly marked.

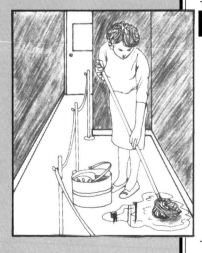

There is a list of further guidance material at the back of the book.

DESIGN FOR HEALTH

- seats and benches at a sensible height, and lifting aids to reduce back injuries

- seats of suitable design, construction and dimensions with a back rest supporting the small of the back and, if needed, a foot rest

- machine controls and instruments designed and arranged for best control and posture

- engineering controls, like local exhaust ventilation systems, to reduce health risks from dangerous substances and noise

- special tools and good design of working areas to reduce hand and forearm injury caused by repetitive movements

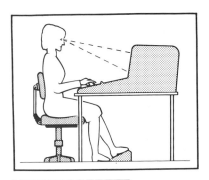

A SAFE PLACE TO WORK

- adequate space for easy movement and safe machine adjustment

- no tripping hazards (trailing wires etc)

- handholds or guardrails where people might fall from floor edges

- emergency provisions eg life belts/jackets for work near water; means of escape from freezer rooms

- no glass, except 'safety glass', in spring doors and on busy gangways

- neat and tidy storage of tools

- furniture placed so that sharp corners don't present a hazard to passers-by.

LIGHTING

- good general illumination with no glare

- regular cleaning and maintenance of lights and windows

- local lighting for dangerous processes and to reduce eye strain and fatigue

- no flickering from fluorescent tubes (it can be dangerous with some rotating machinery)

- adequate emergency lighting

- specially constructed fittings for flammable or explosive atmospheres eg during paint spraying

- outside areas satisfactorily lit for work and access during hours of darkness for security as well as safety

- light coloured wall finishes to improve brightness, or darker colours to reduce arc welding flash, for example.

Prohibition Don't Do	**Warning** Risk of Danger	**Safe Condition** The Safe Way	**Mandatory** Must do

COMFORT

- comfortable working temperature - usually above 16 °C (60°F) for sedentary occupations

- suitable clothing in high or low temperatures (eg freezer rooms) or a heated rest room (eg tyre changing premises)

- good ventilation (avoiding draughts) particularly in high humidity

- mechanical ventilation where fresh air supply is insufficient

- an easily read thermometer in the workroom

- heating systems should not give off fumes into the workplace

- noise levels controlled to reduce nuisance as well as damage to health

- heat stress reduced by controlling radiant heat (especially near head level) and local 'hot spots'.

Health hazards - from maintenance or building work as well as production processes - may be less obvious than safety hazards, but their results can be just as serious. Providing ready access to treatment and promoting improved general health can have benefits all round.

The references on these pages are described more fully in the publications list at the back of the book.

WORK RELATED DISEASES

People at work can encounter a wide range of substances capable of damaging their health. Many substances are used directly in industrial processes; others arise naturally (eg fungal spores). Some arise in service functions (eg cleaning) and others are given off as by-products of processes.

The Control of Substances Hazardous to Health Regulations 1988 (COSHH Regulations) cover virtually all substances hazardous to health. Only asbestos, lead, materials producing ionising radiations and substances below ground in mines, which have their own legislation, are excluded.

Basic principles of occupational hygiene underlie the COSHH Regulations:

- assess the risk to health arising from work and what precautions are needed

- introduce appropriate measures to prevent or control the risk

- ensure that control measures are used and that equipment is properly maintained and procedures observed

- where necessary, monitor the exposure of workers and carry out an appropriate form of surveillance of their health

- inform, instruct and train employees about the risks and the precautions to be taken.

See: IND(G)64(L); IND(G)65(L); IND(G)67(L)

HEALTH SURVEILLANCE

Health surveillance may be required by law for some jobs.

A doctor or nurse from the Employment Medical Advisory Service (EMAS) or an EMAS Appointed Doctor will carry out medical surveillance for commercial diving, certain work with asbestos insulation or other hazardous substances.

A suitably trained person could carry out health surveillance in some cases - eg inspection for dermatitis. Special conditions apply to some people particularly at risk, such as pregnant women (or those who might bear children) working with hazards like lead or ionising radiations.

FITNESS FOR WORK

People's physical capacities vary. Some tasks (HGV driving, steel erecting, diving) place particular physical demands on workers, and individuals need to be specially selected and trained for these jobs.

Other people may have health problems which affect their ability to do normal jobs. Many employees find their capacity for work temporarily reduced by illness or injury. Those returning to work after a period of sickness are likely to need help in readjusting to their jobs.

Workers must be physically and mentally suited to their jobs. It is usually possible to anticipate and resolve problems by seeking specialist advice.

HEALTH PROBLEMS 7

INFECTION

Biological agents like bacteria and viruses can cause disease and illness by:
- infecting the body when they are inhaled (breathed in), ingested (swallowed), or when they penetrate the skin

- causing allergic or intolerant reactions in people sensitive to them.

Work with human pathogens or genetic manipulation is not the only way of meeting microbiological hazards. Other examples are:

- Legionnaire's Disease - found in many recirculating and hot water systems such as air conditioning plant, cooling towers, industrial sprays and showers
- rodent-borne infections such as leptospirosis, which occurs amongst fish farmers and scrapyard workers
- infections through blood contact - a risk in some occupations eg hairdressing, tattooing
- diseases transmitted by living or dead animals - to farmers and petshop workers for instance
- diseases like anthrax carried in animal products such as pelts, skins and wool.

Most biological risks can be reduced by simple control methods. Sometimes immunisation may be needed.

See: GN:EH 23; IAC(L)27
Department of Employment leaflet (PL 811) - AIDS (Acquired Immune Deficiency Syndrome): AIDS in Employment.

MEDICATION AND ALCOHOL

Taking medicines (on prescription or otherwise) can affect people's ability to work safely. For example drugs prescribed for hay fever can cause drowsiness.

Many accidents at work are caused by the effects of alcohol. Even slight intoxication can lead to loss of concentration and can result in serious injury if machinery or vehicles are operated.

Abuse of drugs or substances such as solvents (glue sniffing) can also cause accidents at work. Be on the lookout for vulnerable people.
See: OP 1

SPECIAL HAZARDS

Some chemicals (and other agents, such as radiations) can have serious long-term effects on health. Symptoms may not appear at once - with asbestos and ionising radiations the effects of exposure may only become apparent years or decades later.

Make sure that you and your workforce are informed about special hazards which may arise at your workplace, and that you take the right precautions.

WHERE TO GET HELP

If in doubt get expert advice. EMAS offers help with work related health problems and advice on general health promotion at work. It can also put you in touch with other sources of advice. Contact EMAS at area offices of HSE.

VISUAL DISPLAY
UNITS (VDUs)

Long periods of use may result in headaches, eye strain and back problems. Well designed work areas, comfortable seating and a properly adjusted screen should minimise these symptoms. There is no evidence at present that users of VDUs need to take special precuations to protect against radiation emissions.
See: IND(G)36(L)

UPPER LIMB
DISORDERS

Many employees - including assemblers, supermarket checkout assistants and keyboard operators - are affected by upper limb disorders at some point in their working lives.

The term covers a number of related medical conditions (including tenosynovitis, carpal tunnel syndrome, tennis elbow and beat conditions) which affect the arms, particularly the hands and forearms. The symptoms of upper limb disorders include pain or soreness and limited movement of affected parts. Typical causes are incorrect posture, too great a workload, over-forceful movements, and inadequate rest periods.

Injury can be prevented by improved design of working areas (position of keyboard and VDU screens, heights of workbenches and chairs, lighting), adjustments of workloads and rest periods, provision of special tools, and better training and supervision.

If untreated, upper limb disorders can be seriously disabling.

8 SAFE USE OF CHEMICALS

Poor working practices with chemicals may have a rapid and serious effect on health, or cause chronic diasabling diseases after repeated exposure. Some forms of ill health, such as cancer, take years to develop. The risks may be increased by the stress of working in noisy or hot environments follow these guidelines ...

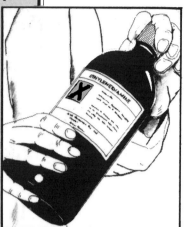

ASSESS THE RISKS

Before using a toxic substance consider its possible ill effects and find out how it can be handled safely. Read the 'supply label' on the package and the supplier's hazard data sheet to identify hazardous components - you can then assess the risks as they apply in your workplace and in the way you use the substance. Find out about:

- the hazards of the ingredients in, or formed from, the substance

- how it affects the body when breathed in, swallowed or absorbed through the skin

- the consequences of short- or long-term exposure

- the concentration or conditions likely to cause ill health

- the first symptoms of overexposure.

Then decide whether the hazardous substance can be removed from use, substituted or controlled by other means. The precautions you take must match the risk. They will depend on the substance, the quantities involved and the way it is used (Control of Substances Hazardous to Health Regulations 1988)

Examples of specific controls:

- workers handling lead may not eat, drink or smoke in the workplace. (Control of Lead at Work Regulations 1980)

- workers handling dangerous chemicals in factory premises must wear approved eye protection. (Protection of Eyes Regulations 1974)

Similar rules may apply to you- if in doubt, err on the side of caution. You can often reduce risks by using a safer substitute.

Make sure relevant inform- ation is available to people handling the substance or likely to get involved in dealing with spillage

DON'T GET POISONED!

- do not smoke, eat or drink in chemical handling areas, and do not keep food there
- do not siphon or pipette by mouth - use a pump or manually-primed siphon
- do not transfer contamination eg by putting pens and pencils in your mouth. Wash hands before leaving the workplace
- do not store chemicals in containers such as milk bottles or jam jars; make sure labels are not damaged, removed or obliterated
- do prevent poisoning through the skin - use gloves with many hairdressing preparations, for instance
- do keep dangerous materials in a locked place and maintain a record of their use and stock level

Control of Lead at Work Regulations 1980
See: Approved COP
Control of Substances Hazardous to Health Regulations 1988
See: Leaflets: IND(G)64(L), IND(G)67(L), IND(G)65(L)
Protection of Eyes Regulations 1974

The references on these pages are described more fully in the publications list at the back of the book.

CASE STUDY

Workers at a small factory making soft drinks developed rashes on their hands and arms. The neck and face of one person was affected. Dermatitis was caused by food additive ingredients (colours, flavours etc) in the product. Sometimes the powder in the air caused people to have nose bleeds. One woman developed asthma and bronchitis.

SKIN CONTAMINATION

Some substances can poison by being absorbed directly through the skin; others cause skin problems. Many workers experience such skin problems, of which dermatitis is the most common.

Dermatitis is caused by exposure to chemicals (as well as to abrasives, certain living organisms, ultra-violet radiation and heat). Mineral oil, soluble cutting oils and solvents such as paraffin, trichloroethylene and white spirit are irritant. Chrome and nickel compounds, some resins and their hardeners, some woods and plants cause skin allergy.

Dermatitis occurs in a wide range of work activities and can have serious effects on health. If the causes are not investigated and dealt with, employees may have to leave their jobs.

Corrective action need not be difficult or expensive. It may involve relatively minor changes in processes or substances used, better protective clothing, or training employees in better working practices and skin care. Specialist advice may sometimes be needed to find out the cause of dermatitis - EMAS can advise on how to obtain it.

Precautions include:

- limiting contact with known skin irritants and allergens by adopting safe working practices or changes to processes

- using gloves which are impermeable to the material concerned avoiding contamination of the inside of the gloves

- frequently washing gloves and other protective items - especially before removal - to prevent the spread of contamination

- washing the skin when contamination does occur

- using reconditioning creams (and sometimes also barrier creams)

- seeking medical advice if the skin becomes red and flaky, or begins to blister or crack. Usually rashes are relatively easy to control with treatment.

See: SHW 355, 366, 367, 397; GN:EH 26; MS(B)6

FIRST AID

Know how to deal with accidents involving chemicals. Sometimes you need special first aid items readily available, for example when handling cyanides or hydrofluoric acid. Follow your supplier's advice.

See: MS(B)7

PROTECTIVE CLOTHING

Use of protective clothing should be a last resort after other means of control have been fully considered.

Take your supplier's advice when choosing clothing and gloves. Many solvents quickly penetrate rubber-based materials. Few materials provide protection if immersed in hazardous chemicals - design work methods so that at worst only minor splashes occur.

Keep protective clothing clean to avoid irritation from materials, like cement, which may enter gloves at the wrist. Contaminated clothing should always be cleaned, eg washed or hosed down, before the operator takes it off - this will prevent contamination the next time it is worn.

Disposable suits are useful for dirty jobs where unit laundry costs are high eg for visitors required to wear protective clothing.

Eye protection and respirators should be suitable for the purposes and respirators should be of a type approved by HSE or conforming to an HSE approved standard.

HOW TO TACKLE THE PROBLEM

This list shows the preferred order of controlling the risk. Many situations need a combination of control measures.

1 **SUBSTITUTION** - use a safer substance or process

2 **ISOLATION** - of the dangerous chemical from operators

3 **ENCLOSURE OF THE PROCESS** - to prevent operators or other workers being exposed

4 **LOCAL EXHAUST VENTILATION** - to remove toxic fume or dust at source

5 **GENERAL VENTILATION** with fresh air

6 **GOOD HOUSEKEEPING** to minimise accidental contact

7 **MINIMISING THE TIME OF EXPOSURE** or the number of people exposed

8 **TRAINING** in the use of engineering controls

9 **PERSONAL PROTECTIVE CLOTHING AND EQUIPMENT**

10 **GOOD WELFARE FACILITIES** to aid high standards of personal hygiene

11 **HEALTH SURVEILLANCE** to detect early signs of ill health

Substances are often most dangerous when breathed in. Harmful material should be removed from the air to make it safe to breathe. This section looks at how you can control problems created by dust, smoke, vapour, fume, mist, spray and gas.

The reference on these pages are described more fully in the publications list at the back of the book.

LIMITING EXPOSURE

Dangerous dust is not always visible. Very small particles which you may not be able to see can enter deep in the lungs and may be absorbed into the body, causing scarring or even cancer.

Controlling the amount of dust or vapour in a worker's 'breathing zone' usually involves reducing it to the lowest level which is reasonably practicable. For dusts and a wide range of specified substances, limits to exposure have been laid down and are listed in Guidance Note EH 40 *Occupational exposure limits.*

These limits are not dividing lines between 'safe' and 'not safe'. For some substances, such as most carcinogens (ie cancer-causing agents), ill effects may result after low level short period exposure.

In some cases occupational hygienists may be needed to measure workers' exposure to toxic materials and to check that the limits are not being exceeded. They use 'air sampling' techniques. The way it is done, and the significance of the result, need careful thought. Your inspector may be able to help.

Sampling may also be necessary to confirm the absence of short-term hazards eg before allowing workers to enter tanks or vessels in which there might be a contaminent or oxygen deficiency.

LOCAL EXHAUST VENTILATION (LEV)

A local exhaust ventilation (LEV) system sucks dust or vapour through a small hood or a ventilated booth and takes it away from the worker.

The system should:

- extract dust or vapour as close as possible to its source

- control contamination of the work area below the exposure limit of the particular material

SOME TIPS FOR HANDLING DUSTY MATERIALS

- prevent dust entering the workroom by enclosing the process
- clear up spillages quickly
- have smooth work surfaces to allow easy cleaning
- clean regularly and systematically using a dust-free method such as a vacuum system with a high efficiency filter
- keep dusty materials in covered containers
- do not allow pastes or drips to dry out
- substitute with dust free materials eg pellets
- prevent the body and underclothing getting contaminated - cover the head and neck
- have overalls which are tight fitting at wrist and ankle

- suck air away from the breathing zone, not through it

- have an adequate air flow - at least 1 m/s - at the source of the pollutant

- have sufficient air flow inside ducts to prevent dust being deposited inside and blocking them

- have ductwork with gently angled bends and junctions, and tapered diameter changes.

All ventilation equipment needs to be inspected, examined and tested regularly by a competent person. Proper checks include measuring the air velocity or the pressures in the system, or air sampling in the workroom. In some industries examinations required are laid down by law but all LEV should be examined and tested at least once every 14 months.

Air from exhaust systems needs special cleaning if it is recirculated inside the building. Make sure that exhaust systems do not vent where contaminants can get back into the working areas through rooflights or windows. If air cleaning is necessary to protect the outside environment, your inspector can tell you who to contact. See: HS(G)37

WHERE YOU MIGHT FIND CONTAMINATION

Dust can arise, for example, during weighing of powdery materials, bag filling, the handling of dusty or damaged bags, or even when a person wearing contaminated clothing moves about. Vapour is given off from any wet surface by evaporation, and the amount increases enormously if the liquid is sprayed or heated.

Look carefully at your processes and consult the suppliers of the substances you use.

Here are examples of possible hazards and how they might arise.

	Hazardous substance	Source	Process	Possible effect
DUST	Silica (clay)	Dry sweeping	Pottery	Silicosis
	Hardwood	Sanding	Furniture	Nasal cancer
	Spore	Mouldy hay	Farming	Farmer's lung
FUME	Zinc	Hot flame	Flamecutting	Fume fever
	Cadmium	Heat	Hard solder	Emphysema
VAPOUR	Perchloroethylene	Evaporation	Dry cleaning	Liver damage
	Isocyanate	Moulding	Plastics	Asthma
GAS	Nitrogen oxides	Hot flame	Welding	Lung irritation
	Carbon monoxide	Engine exhaust	Garage	Deoxygenation
	Slurry gases	Fermentation	Farming	Asphyxiation
MIST AND SPRAY	Chromic acid	Bubbles bursting	Plating	Ulceration
	Non-solvent refined mineral oil	Machine lubrication	Engineering	Skin cancer
	Animal infection	Meat handling	Abattoir	Brucellosis

GAS APPLIANCES

Gas appliances, whether bottle or mains supplied, use up oxygen in the air and produce highly toxic carbon monoxide if the gas doesn't burn properly. They need plenty of fresh air to work efficiently and safely. Check that the room has adequate ventilation, that air inlets are not blocked to prevent draughts and that flues and chimneys are not obstructed. Have gas appliances installed, regularly serviced and repaired by a competent person.

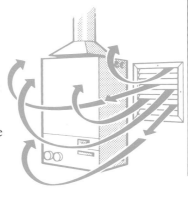

RESPIRATORY PROTECTIVE EQUIPMENT

Where problems cannot be eliminated or controlled by engineering methods you may have to rely on respirators. Make sure the type you choose is right for the job. Vapour-type filters are not generally suitable for dusts - and vise-versa.
Respirators should be suitable for the purpose and be of a type approved by HSE or conform within HSE approved standard. Respirators must not be used where there is a shortage of oxygen.

 Blue, brown and white asbestos may be found in buildings as heat and noise insulation or in fire protection materials. All types of asbestos are dangerous and the colour can often be misleading. Products containing asbestos carry a warning label. Specific legal controls on asbestos include:

- prohibition on work with insulation or coating except by an HSE licence holder (Asbestos (Licensing) Regulation 1983)

- precautions necessary when it is handled (Control of Asbestos at Work Regulations 1987)

- prohibition of import and supply (including second hand articles) and use of blue and brown asbestos (Asbestos (Prohibitions) Regulations 1985)

If you use asbestos it is essential to discuss the work with your inspector.

See: GN:EH 10, 35, 36, 37, 41
IND(G)17(L); IND(G)54(L); IND(S)23(C)

Asbestos (Licensing) Regulations 1983
See: HS(R)19

Control of Asbestos at Work Regulations 1987
See: COP 21

Asbestos (Prohibitions) Regulations 1985.

CASE STUDY

A garage owner sprayed two car doors and next day spent two minutes spraying a car roof with paint containing isocyanate hardener. While working he experienced shortness of breath with chest tightness. He became worse and was taken to hospital but died after three days. Even for such short-term exposure protective equipment and adequate ventilation should have been provided.

See: GN:EH 16

10 NOISE AND VIBRATION

Excessive noise is a major health hazard. It accelerates the normal hearing loss which occurs as we grow older. Less obvious side effects - increased pulse rate, blood pressure and breathing rate - indicate that noise and vibration cause stress.

VIBRATION

Vibration is often associated with noise and may sometimes be reduced by using shock absorbing materials eg as machine mountings or 'damping' on non-reverberating linings. Direct vibration, through a vibrating floor to the feet or from vibrating tools to the hands, can damage bones and joints. A condition known as 'vibration white finger' is caused by an impaired blood supply to the fingers. Much vibration can be reduced by proper installation, maintenance and use but although you can take the obvious precautions, like fitting hand tools with vibration-absorbing handles, a full solution to a vibration problems often requires expert help.

See: GN:PM 31

The references on these pages are described more fully in the publications list at the back of the book.

NOISE AT WORK

The Noise at Work Regulations are intended to reduce hearing damage caused by loud noise. They require employers to take action when noise reaches the 85 dB(A) 'First Action Level' and further action if it reaches 90 dB(A) 'Second' or 140 dB 'Peak' Action Levels.

- Assess noise levels - at the First Action Level get noise assessed by a competent person and keep a record - you can find out roughly whether levels are around 85 dB(A) by checking if you can hear clearly what someone is saying when they are two metres away.

- Information for workers - at the First Action Level you need to inform your workers about the risks to their hearing and that you will provide ear protectors if wanted - if any of your workers thinks their hearing is being affected, suggest they take medical advice.

- Control noise exposure if noise reaches the Second or Peak Action Levels, you must do all that is reasonably practicable to reduce it - mark zones where levels reach the Second or Peak Action Levels with the recognised signs to restrict entry.

- Ear protectors (ear muffs or ear plugs) when exposures reach the First Action Level, provide ear protectors if workers want them - make sure everyone wears ear protectors in areas where noise reaches the Second or Peak Action Levels and in marked zones.

- Makers and suppliers of machinery etc should provide noise data with their equipment if levels are likely to reach the First or Peak Action Levels. If you are buying machinery insist on this information.

ACTION LEVELS

- First Action Level 85 dB(A).

- Second Action Level 90 dB(A).

These are 'personal daily noise exposure' levels, sometimes called daily 'noise dose' and denoted '$L_{EP,d}$'. The dose depends on the noise level(s) in the work area and how long people spend there during their working day.

- Peak Action Level 200 pascals (equivalent to 140 dB re 20 µPa) is the peak pressure reached by the sound wave, eg where loud impulse sources such as cartridge-operated tools are used even occasionally.

CONTROL OF NOISE

Protection against noise is best achieved by controlling it at source. Follow this sequence to reduce exposure - wearing protection is very much a last resort:

- design the machine and process to produce less noise
- choose quiet machines or processes when selecting production methods. Get the supplier to specify noise levels at the operators' positions
- enclose noisy machines with sound-insulating panels
- put noisy machines and processes in separate rooms or fix ceiling high partitions
- fit silencers on exhaust systems
- get operators in noisy areas to wear ear protection
- reduce the duration of exposure by job rotation or provide a noise refuge.

CHECKLIST

- are noisy machines/processes identified by warning signs?

- does everyone in a noisy area need to work there? Perhaps some jobs could be moved somewhere quieter

  how long can people stay within the noisy area without their noise 'dose' exceeding the Second Action Level?

- have employees been warned about the dangers of noise and instructed in the use of hearing protectors?

- do the ear protectors give adequate protection for the level and type of noise?

- has the manufacturer's information about noise levels been checked by actual measurements when the job is going on?

- how will changes in work methods or machine wear affect noise levels?

- are loose panels or unbalanced rotating parts contributing to noise and vibration?

- would better maintenance or a slower running speed reduce noise levels?

EAR PROTECTION

Don't rely too heavily on ear protectors. In practice they reduce noise exposure less than is often claimed because they may be uncomfortable or inconvenient to wear. A good fitting plastic foam or mineral down/waxed cotton wool plug, if properly worn, may be as good as ear muffs, which nominally provide more protection. To be effective, ear protectors need to be worn all the time that people are in noisy places. If they are left off for even short periods even the best protectors cannot greatly reduce noise exposure.

Hearing damage is cumulative. Make sure that young people in particular get into the routine of avoiding noise exposure, before their hearing is permanently damaged.

EXPOSURE TO NOISE

The diagram shows typical noise levels associated with work activities. The bands show the length of time which workers can be exposed to such noise before their 'noise dose' exceeds the Action Levels.

First Action Level

Second Action Level

dB(A)   EXAMPLES

108	hand grinding of metal
105	unsilenced air discharge
102	chain saw
99	circular saw
96	petrol driven grass mower/power press operator
93	sheet metal shop/paint spraying
90	tractor cab maximum
87	electric drill/underground train at full speed
85	plastic injection moulding machine
81	domestic food blender

¼ ½ 1   2   4   8

HOURS

Visible light is just one part of the spectrum of electromagnetic radiation, which ranges from radio waves at one end to ultra-violet light, and beyond to X-rays, at the other. This section looks at the health risks arising from exposure to such electromagnetic radiation, and to radiation from sources of radioactivity.

THE SPECTRUM

This table shows where you are likely to find various types of electromagnetic radiation and identifies some of the hazards they can cause.

Radiation	Emitted from ...	Examples of hazards
Radio frequency and microwaves	Plastics welding, communications, catering, drying and heating equipment	Excessive heating of any exposed parts of the body
Infra-red	Any hot material	Reddening of skin, burns, cataracts
Visible radiation	All visible light sources. High intensity beams, eg lasers, are especially penetrating	Heating and destruction of tissue of the eye or skin
Ultra-violet	Welding, some lasers, mercury vapour lamps, carbon arcs	'Sunburns', conjunctivitis, skin cancer, production of toxic levels of ozone
X-rays and gamma rays (ionising radiations)	X-ray machines, some other electronic equipment, some radiography machines, radio-active 'sources' and substances	Burns, dermatitis, cancer, cell damage or blood changes

ULTRA-VIOLET (UV) LIGHT

Machines emitting ultra-violet (UV) light should normally be in a properly designed and manufactured enclosure, or adequately screened.

Take care to avoid UV light, eg by wearing suitable eye protection.

During welding, for instance, precautions are needed to screen UV radiation from passers-by; welders should use special goggles or a face screen.

Some UV lamps are more dangerous than others. Make sure, particularly when fitting replacements in UV devices, that you choose the correct type specified by the manufacturer.

Insect killing devices with bright UV sources are often found in food premises. They are not hazardous to the eyes in normal use and are usually positioned out of reach.

See: IAC Booklet; GN:GS 18

MICROWAVES AND RADIO FREQUENCIES

Exposure to these radiations should be minimised.

Leakage of energy from microwave ovens is normally very small. Minimise it by keeping microwave ovens well maintained and, in particular, the door seals clean. Make sure the hinges, door latch and safety interlocks on the access door all work properly.

Occupational exposure to stray radio frequency (RF) energy from RF heaters, driers and presses is best minimised by properly designed and installed shielding around the electrode applicator. Systems of work which limit exposure time or approach to the source may also be necessary.

Simple techniques can often reduce the risk of deep-seated burns due to contact with energised RF electrodes. Adequate precautions must be taken to make sure that unauthorised persons can't gain access to the high voltage electrical equipment eg by interlocking all cubicle doors.

See: GN:PM 51

The references on these pages are described more fully in the publications list at the back of the book.

RADIATIONS 11

INFRA-RED

With some 'hot bodies' (like pools of molten metal) protective clothing may be needed to reduce sunburn and irritation of the skin. Eye protection with appropriate filters is often worn to overcome discomfort - and can be essential with some infra-red sources, such as certain lasers.

Low levels of infra-red radiation nuisance - from overhead heating, for example - may be countered by increasing air speed.

LASERS

A laser - a concentrated beam of radiation - can be dangerous whether it is viewed directly or after reflection from a smooth surface. The beam may not always be visible.

Even on low powered lasers it is unwise to view the beam directly. Do not override any interlocks provided.

Maintenance workers who have to examine inside machines may be most at risk. They need to be properly trained and follow a defined system of work which includes use of eye protection.

High powered lasers must only be used with expert advice on safety precautions - which would normally include positioning the device inside a safely interlocked enclosure.

Where lasers are used for display, eg at discotheques, risks to the public may arise - seek expert advice.

See: GN:PM 19

IONISING RADIATIONS

Radioactive substances and 'sources', or any equipment emitting ionising radiations, must be used with great care. Any work involving exposure to ionising radiations should be started only after consultation with your inspector and with full understanding of the legal and safety implications.

Ionising Radiations Regulations 1985 applying to all work activities involving ionising radiations lay down very detailed requirements to keep exposure to a minimum. In particular, before you begin work with ionising radiations or bring any radioactive source onto your premises you must notify your inspector. You may also need authorisation from the radiochemicals inspector of the Department of Environment.

Sometimes the radiation warning sign may be found on small devices like smoke detectors, thickness gauges and static eliminators. Although the risk from these items is almost negligible when they are used properly, find out the rules for their safe use and storage. Never tamper with the containment of such devices, or with luminous articles or self-illuminating devices, because any released radioactivity may enter the body where it is much more harmful than when contained in the article.

Contractors who carry out radiography work (eg checking for weld defects in pipework) have to follow carefully laid down rules to avoid anyone being accidentally exposed to the radiation - whether employee or passer-by. They must notify HSE before the work is started.

See: IND(S)9(L)
Ionising Radiations Regulations 1985; See: COP 16, 23

FOLLOW THE SAFETY RULES

- get safety information from your supplier or other specialist adviser
- identify, mark and (where possible) enclose sources of radiation
- identify and clearly mark all hazard areas
- instruct employees about dangers and precautions, including use of the correct protective equipment
- review safety procedures periodically
- maintain equipment to minimise exposure eg by regular checking of interlocks.

Remember that, for work with ionising radiations, you may need to:

- arrange for medical examinations and routine dose assessments of certain 'classified' employees
- appoint a radiation protection adviser
- have contingency arrangements to cater for spills of radioactive substances, X-ray exposures failing to terminate etc
- get authorisation for use, storage and safe disposal of radioactive substances.

12 ELECTRICITY

Every year about 1000 work accidents involving electric shock or electrical burns are reported to the HSE. About 25 of these are fatal. Many other deaths and injuries result from fires caused by poor electrical standards. Simple commonsense rules can reduce these hazards.

STATIC ELECTRICITY

Many people experience a slight electric shock when they touch a metal door handle after walking across a synthetic carpet. Similar charging can occur during the movement of powders and liquids, sometimes sufficient to cause a spark which will ignite a dust cloud or a flammable vapour. Whenever conveying or pouring organic powders (eg grain, tea dust) or flammable liquids, use metal containers and make sure all metalwork is bonded and earthed. Don't use materials like plastic, which can become charged. For such jobs as electrostatic paint spraying, make sure both the workpiece and anyone in the area are adequately earthed, eg by getting the operator and assistant to wear anti-static footwear.

See: OP 5

ELECTRIC SHOCK

Would you know what to do if someone received an electric shock? Resuscitation needs training and practice. Make sure that as many as possible of your staff receive elementary first aid training. Dispay a copy of the 'electric shock placard' which shows you what to do.

ELECTRIC SHOCK FROM KETTLE KILLS GARDENER

A young gardener received a fatal electric shock whilst filling a kettle with water in a mess room.

The kettle was plugged in and switched on at the time of the accident. It was about five years old but had not been used for some 18 months as an electric water heater had been provided. However, this heater had failed and while waiting for repairs the kettle was taken back into use.

Examination of the kettle lead after the accident showed that the earth wire was not connected to the terminal in the plug and that the insulation had melted at the point where the live and earth wires crossed. The undertaking was fined £1,000 with £50 costs.

AVOID OVERHEAD LINES ...

Electricity can flashover from overhead power lines. Don't work under them or allow any part of a machine (eg crane jib, tipper lorry body) ladder etc within 10 m of a power line without seeking advice.

See: GN:GS 6

... AND UNDERGROUND CABLES

Assume there are buried live electricity cables present before digging holes in the street, pavement or near buildings.

Consult your electricity board if you're likely to be working near overhead lines or buried cables.

See: GN:GS 33

The references on these pages are described more fully in the publications list at the back of the book.

PORTABLE APPARATUS

Electrical tools used outdoors or where there is a lot of earthed metalwork are best worked from a safety isolating transformer or connected through a residual current circuit breaker which will cut off the power quickly if someone gets an electric shock. Lighting can often be supplied at extra-low voltage (12V or 25V). Sometimes the use of electricity can be avoided altogether eg by using pneumatic tools.　　　See: GN:PM 32

SWITCHES AND CONDUIT

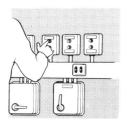

There must be a switch or isolator near each fixed machine to cut off power in an emergency. Power cables to machines should be armoured, covered in thick flexible rubber, PVC or installed in conduit. There must be a good earth connection.

DAMAGE

Protect light bulbs, or other items which may be easily damaged in use.

SOCKETS

Provide enough socket outlets - over loading sockets by using adaptors is a fire hazard. If necessary use an additional multi-plug socket block.

ENVIRONMENT

When used outdoors, in damp or corrosive atmospheres, or where steam or water jets are used, socket outlets should be of special design and may need to be protected by a residual current circuit breaker. Get special advice.

PLUGS

Always use a proper plug with the flex firmly clamped to stop the wires (particularly the earth) pulling out of the terminals. Some tools are double-insulated for extra protection - these have only two wires (neutral and live). Make sure you connect them properly. See: GN:GS 7

CABLE JOINTS

Replace frayed and damaged cables completely. Join lengths in good condition only by using proper connectors or cable couplers.

EXPLOSION PROTECTION

If the atmosphere is particularly dusty or likely to be flammable, dustproof or explosion protected equipment may be needed. Low voltage equipment (eg 12 V) gives no protection against igniting flammable vapours. To choose the correct equipment you need specialist advice.

See: Electricity at Work Regulations 1989; HS(R)25

CHECK THAT...

- plugs, sockets and fittings are obtained from a reputable manufacturer and are sufficiently robust for business use

- fuses, circuit breakers and other devices are correctly rated for the circuit they protect

- access to electrical dangers is prevented - covers are kept closed and (if possible) locked, with the key held by a responsible person

- the main switches are readily accessible and clearly identified, and everyone knows how to use them in an emergency

- electrical installations are checked periodically and repairs carried out by a competent electrician

- all portable apparatus is listed so that it can be regularly inspected and its condition recorded. Don't forget hired or borrowed tools, or equipment such as floor polishers which may be used after premises have closed

- suspect or faulty apparatus is taken out of use, put in a secure place and labelled 'do not use' until attended to by a competent person

- special maintenance requirements of waterproof or explosion-protected equipment have been recorded and someone made responsible for it

- someone is responsible for checking the 'test' button on residual current circuit breakers

- tools and power sockets are switched off before plugging in

- appliances are unplugged before cleaning or making adjustments.

Many serious accidents at work involve machinery. The guarding of dangerous parts of machines has been a legal requirement for many years. Use these guidelines to check that you are using your machines safely.

THE HAZARDS

Guarding requirements have developed to prevent accidents which happen when people get close to dangerous parts of machines. You may not have had an accident on your machinery - but that doesn't mean it is safe.

Learn to recognise dangerous parts and think about how to prevent injury. When checking whether a guard is adequate, consider not only your disciplined and trained workers but also the careless or foolish ones. If you provide a guard which is inconvenient to use or can be easily defeated, you may inadvertently encourage your employees to break the law and risk injury.

When you buy or hire a machine the law requires the supplier to provide necessary safeguards, but you should always check carefully before allowing the machine to be used.

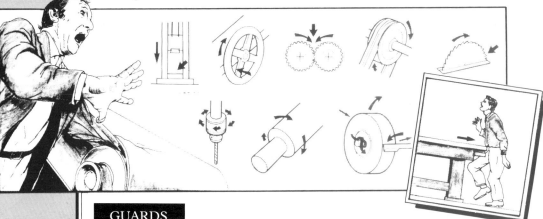

GUARDS

Dangerous parts should either be out of reach, or there should be some safeguard to eliminate or reduce the danger before someone can reach them.

Check that guards are strong enough and, if fixed, that they cannot be too easily removed. If frequent access is needed close to a dangerous part it is probably better to interlock the guard, so that the motor cannot start before the guard is in position and opening the guard stops the machine. Make sure, however, that the interlocking switch or valve is sufficiently robust for the job, and that the way it works makes it difficult (figure A), not easy (figure B), for someone to defeat the interlock.

A wide range of interlocks are available - you may, for example, want a guard with its own key (figure C), or one which can be used in wet conditions (figure D).

Occasionally trip systems such as photo-electric safety systems, pressure sensitive mats or automatic guards may be more appropriate than fixed or interlocking guards. Sometimes, where inertia of the machinery produces dangerous overrun after the power has been disconnected, mechanical restraints or timing devices are necessary. In all these applications you may need specialist advice.

There is a list of further guidance material at the back of the book.

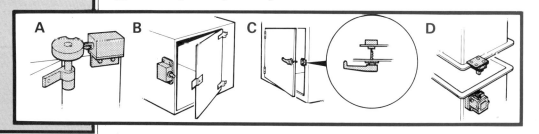

DANGEROUS MACHINES

There are special rules for some machines used in offices, agriculture and industry ...

Some are 'prescribed dangerous machines' which young people can use only after full instruction and sufficient training, and under close supervision. Examples include guillotines, mixers, bacon and vegetable slicers, power operated wrappers and slicers.

Some - such as abrasive wheels, woodworking machines, horizontal milling machines, and power take-off shafts - are covered by regulations which require particular standards of guarding.

Regulations may require other actions, such as periodic examination of power press guards by a competent person.

Make sure you are providing the guards and any other precautions required by law. Don't allow children to operate, or to help someone to use, a dangerous machine.

Some examples ...

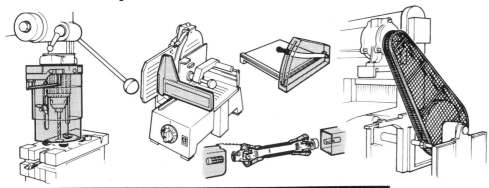

SAFETY DOES NOT STOP WITH THE GUARD

- make sure the guards and other safety devices are regularly checked and maintained in effective working order
- be alert for anyone defeating or getting around guards or safety devices
- consider the best materials for the guard - plastic allows good visibility but may be easily damaged
- machines in premises used by the public should be positioned well away from customers
- ensure control switches are clearly marked to indicate their effect and which machine they control
- is protection really effective? - 'two-hand' control will protect only the operator, not anyone else in the area
- make sure the guards are robust, kept in position and effective - even during cleaning
- if maintenance workers need to remove guards or other safety devices make sure they are protected by some other means
- identify risks from electrical, hydraulic or pneumatic power supplies
- check that emergency cut-off switches, eg mushroom head push buttons, are coloured red and within easy reach
- make sure controls are designed and placed to avoid unintentional operation eg shrouded start buttons and pedals
- train operators to work machines safely and provide them with protective clothing
- safety check the plant before first use and after modifications.

For further information ...

British Standard BS 5304 *Safety of Machinery* is a useful guide. It illustrates machinery hazards and methods of safeguarding them. Your supplier or machine manufacturer should also be able to advise you. There are several HSE publications on machinery safety.

OPERATOR'S
CHECKLIST

Check every time that ...

- you know how to stop the machine before you start it
- all fixed guards are fitted correctly and all mechanical guards are working
- all materials to be used are clear of working parts of the machine
- the area around the machine is clean, tidy and free from obstruction
- your supervisor is told at once if you think a machine is not working properly
- you are wearing appropriate protective clothing and equipment, such as safety glasses or safety shoes.

Never ...

- use a machine unless you are authorised and trained to do so
- attempt to clean a machine in motion - switch if off and unplug it
- use a machine or appliance which has a danger sign or tag attached. Danger signs should be removed only by an authorised person who is satisfied that the machine or process is safe
- wear dangling chains, loose clothing, gloves, rings or long hair which could get caught up in moving parts
- distract people who are using machines.

Many materials burn rapidly and the fumes and smoke produced - particularly from burning synthetic material, including plastics - may be deadly.

Make sure the means of escape and other general fire precautions are correct and, if necessary, get a 'fire certificate' from your local fire brigade or fire authority. Your inspector can advise you about the fire risks in your processes.

Fire door
Keep shut

The references on these pages are described more fully in the publications list at the back of the book.

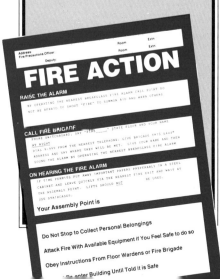

FIRE ACTION

Address:
Fire Precautions Officer: Room   Extn
Deputy   Room   Extn

RAISE THE ALARM
BY OPERATING THE NEAREST BREAKGLASS FIRE ALARM CALL POINT DO NOT BE AFRAID TO SHOUT "FIRE" TO SUMMON AID AND WARN OTHERS

CALL FIRE BRIGADE
PHONE SWITCHBOARD, SAY "FIRE____" STATE FLOOR AND YOUR NAME
AT NIGHT
DIAL 9-999 FROM THE NEAREST TELEPHONE, GIVE BRIGADE THIS NUMBER
_____ AND SAY WHERE THEY WILL BE MET. GIVE YOUR NAME AND THEN
SOUND THE ALARM BY OPERATING THE NEAREST BREAKGLASS FIRE ALARM

ON HEARING THE FIRE ALARM
IF TIME PERMITS PUT AWAY IMPORTANT PAPERS PREFERABLY IN A STEEL CABINET AND LEAVE QUICKLY VIA THE NEAREST FIRE EXIT AND WAIT AT THE ASSEMBLY POINT. LIFTS SHOULD NOT _____ BE USED. USE STAIRCASES.

Your Assembly Point is

Do Not Stop to Collect Personal Belongings
Attack Fire With Available Equipment if You Feel Safe to do so
Obey Instructions From Floor Wardens or Fire Brigade
___ Re-enter Building Until Told it is Safe

STOP FIRE STARTING ...

- where possible use materials which are less flammable, for example solvents with a high flash point; furnishing made of fire resistant materials
- minimise the quantities of flammable materials kept at your workplace and in store
- store flammable material safely, well away from hazardous processes or materials and, where appropriate, from buildings and perimeter boundaries
- warn people of the fire risk by a conspicuous sign at each workplace, storage area and on each container
- some items, like oil-soaked rags, may ignite spontaneously. Keep them in a metal container away from other flammable material
- before welding and similar work remove or insulate flammable material and have fire extinguishers to hand
- control ignition sources, eg naked flames and sparks, and make sure that 'no smoking' rules are obeyed
- make sure that vandals don't have access to flammable waste materials
- remove grease frequently from ducts (such as kitchen ventilators) and cooker extractor hoods.

... AND PREVENT IT SPREADING

- after each spell of work, check the area for smouldering matter or fire
- burn rubbish in a suitable container well away from buildings. Have fire extinguishers on hand. Don't burn aerosol cans and don't 'brighten' fires with flammable liquids
- never wedge open fire-resistant doors designed to stop the spread of fire and smoke
- check that fire dampers inducting and hoods operate efficiently
- if a wall is meant to be fire-resisting, fire-stop any holes, eg around pipe-work, and make sure walls don't finish at a false ceiling

- have enough extinguishers, of the right type and properly maintained, to deal promptly with small outbreaks of fire. Where there is a risk of clothing catching fire, eg in kitchens, provide a suitable fire blanket
- make sure staff know how to raise the alarm and, if necessary, how to use the extinguishers.

MAKE SURE EVERYONE CAN GET OUT SAFELY

- everyone must know what to do in the case of fire. Have a fire drill periodically and display fire action instructions
- make sure there are enough fire exits for everyone to escape quickly, and keep fire doors and escape routes unobstructed and clearly marked
- make sure fire escape doors can be opened easily from the inside whenever anyone is on the premises
- if there is a fire alarm, check weekly that it works and that it can be heard everywhere over normal background noise.

See: General Fire Precautions - Home Office booklets:
Guides to the Fire Precautions Act 1971

HIGHLY FLAMMABLE LIQUIDS

- keep only small quantities (not more than 50 litres) on their own in a metal cupboard or bin for immediate use at the workplace, and larger stocks in a fire-resisting store with spillage retention and good ventilation

- keep containers closed to stop vapour escaping. Where possible use special safety containers which have self-closing lids and caps - contain spillages (eg by dispensing over a tray). Have absorbent material readily available to soak up spillages. Keep contaminated material in a lidded metal bin. Empty it regularly and dispose of its contents safely

- exclude sources of ignition - static electricity, unprotected electrical equipment, cigarettes and naked flames - especially when spraying highly flammable liquids

- dispense and use flammable liquids in a safe place with adequate natural or mechanical ventilation

- treat any drum which has held a flammable substance in just the same way as you would a full one. Never heat it or leave it near a heating appliance

- you may need a licence from your local authority to keep even quite small quantities (eg 15 litres) of petrol or petroleum mixtures. See: GN:CS 2, 15; GN:EH 7, 9; HS(G) 3, 4, 5

FLAMMABLE GAS CYLINDERS

- store full and empty cylinders in a safe, well ventilated place, preferably outside buildings
- never keep cylinders below ground level or next to drains, basements and other low-lying places - heavy gases will not disperse easily

- some gas cylinders, eg acetylene, contain liquid - store them with their valves uppermost

- if appliances aren't moved around, position cylinders outside buildings wherever possible, and pipe gas inside through fixed pipework and individual gas taps on each appliance

- make sure that rooms where appliances are used have sufficient high and low level ventilation which is never blocked up to prevent draughts

- protect cylinders from damage eg by chaining unstable cylinders in racks or on special trolleys

- minimise damage by using the correct hoses, clamps, couplers and regulators for the particular gas and appliance

- turn off cylinder valves at the end of each day's work

- change cylinders away from sources of ignition, in a well ventilated place

- minimise welding flame 'flash-back' into the hoses or cylinders by training operators in correct lighting up and working procedures, and by fitting effective non-return valves and flame arresters

- use soap or detergent/water solution never a flame - to test for leaks.

See: GN:CS 4, 6, 8

FLAMMABLE AND

UNSTABLE SOLIDS

Materials like nitrocellulose and some peroxides can ignite through friction or impact. Non-sparking tools may be needed when scraping deposits from spray booths. Polyurethane (plastic) foam is a well known risk. Follow the supplier's storage rules.

See: GN:CS 17; GN:GS 3; HS(G)1

OXYGEN

Common materials may burn violently at high temperature in the presence of oxygen. Never use oxygen to 'sweeten' the atmosphere. Make sure there are no leaks, especially in confined areas. Don't use oxygen to operate compressed air equipment. Keep oxygen cylinders free from grease and other combustible materials. Don't store them with fuel gases or flammable materials.

See: HSE 8

Given the right conditions, many substances will burn violently or explode. This section looks at situations where an explosion might be more likely than a fire, or where an explosion might be caused by excessive pressure in plant or equipment.

The references on these pages are described more fully in the publications list at the back of the book.

PRESSURE EXPLOSIONS

Any closed system or container under pressure may burst violently. Here's how to reduce the chances of anyone being killed or injured ...

With designed pressure systems - slurry tankers, boilers, air receivers and autoclaves:

- know the safe working pressure of the system
- fit safety valves to relieve excess pressure
- make over- or under-pressurisation unlikely. Fit safety devices such as boiler low water level alarms and reducing valves
- test and examine plant and safety devices regularly.

See: The Pressure Systems and Transportable Gas Containers Regulations 1989 COP 37, 38; IND(S)27(L); GN:PM 4, 5

Avoid accidentally pressurising containers:

- provide boiler 'blow-down' tanks with an adequately sized vent pipe
- cold cut sealed containers, especially any tank which has contained flammable material
- store compressed gas cylinders well away from flammable materials. Mark the storeroom to warn the fire brigade in the event of a fire.

See: IND(G)35(L); GN:PM 60

When using pressure, do so in a controlled way:

- use a tyre cage when inflating vehicle tyres
- deflate tyres before removing divided rim wheels
- pressure test pipes, tanks etc hydraulically rather than with air.

See: GN:GS 4; SHW 428

Avoid risk of violent vaporisation:

- dry all equipment when handling molten metal or using molten salt baths.

See: SHW 849

Do not exert pressure by overspeeding machinery:

- mark grinding machines with the spindle speed and use only abrasive wheels of a higher maximum speed. Wheels must be correctly mounted by a trained person. Keep wheel guards in position.

See: GN:PM 22; HS(G)17

CASE STUDIES

1 An empty oil drum being used as a work bench by a man doing welding exploded when the heat caused residues to vaporise and ignite.

2 An LPG cylinder attached to a portable heater was left overnight in a workman's hut. The hut exploded the following day when a man entered and lit a cigarette. The cylinder may have leaked or the heater been left on overnight, and the flame was extinguished (letting unburned gas escape) because the hut was badly ventilated.

3 A welder was killed while working on a dust collector at a grain store. Heat from the welding torch caused dust inside the collector to explode.

4 Two people were injured in an explosion at a machine which was grinding and chopping waste polystyrene.

5 A man died when spraying highly flammable liquid in a confined space. An explosion was caused by an unprotected light bulb igniting vapours.

MAINS GAS

Gas Safety (Installation and Use) Regulations 1984 covering the installation and use of gas fittings require you to:

- get a competent fitter to install or repair your appliances
- not use a gas appliance which you know or suspect is unsafe
- turn off the gas supply as soon as you suspect a leak and notify your gas supplier at once if gas continues to escape
- not turn the gas on again until the leak has been dealt with.

If you can't turn off the gas at the meter or if after turning it off the smell is still very strong, evacuate the building, contact your gas supplier and tell the police. Do not check for leaks with a naked flame.

DUST EXPLOSIONS

Many dusts form a flammable cloud which will explode when ignited. A small explosion in a plant may disturb accumulation of dust to create a larger flammable cloud which could lead to a secondary explosion severe enough to destroy the building.

Use this checklist if your processes create dust:

- is the dust flammable?

- keep plant dust-tight and frequently checked and cleaned

- keep accumulations of dust to a minimum

- reduce the number of ledges and horizontal surfaces on which dust may settle

- use exhaust ventilation with suitable dust collectors as necessary

- exercise close control over sources of heat such as welding, space heaters, smoking, and overheated bearings

- reduce sparking by using suitable (eg dust-tight) electrical equipment, by earthing sources of static electricity and by excluding tramp metal

- take suitable explosion protection measures. You could, for example, provide explosion vents and a plant structure strong enough to withstand an explosion

- make sure explosion vents discharge safely

- where necessary, minimise the effects of an explosion by using lightweight construction for buildings which house dangerous plant.

Examples of hazardous materials: aluminium powder; flour; bone meal; cotton fly; paper dust; polystyrene; sawdust.

See: SHW 830

GAS- AND OIL- FIRED PLANT

Serious explosions occur in gas- and oil-fired plant such as ovens, stoves and boilers. They are caused by ignition of unburned fuel or of flammable vapours given off when heating articles.

Make sure the operator is fully trained and has a safe system of work for purging, lighting up and shutting down the plant.

In most cases explosion relief and flame failure protection should be fitted.

Except in special cases, make sure there is enough air for the fuel to burn properly and sufficient ventilation to remove the combustion products and any solvents give off. Sometimes interlocks between the heat source and ventilation will be necessary.

See: HS(G)16

EXPLOSIVES AND EXPLOSIVE PROPERTIES

Specific controls apply to most explosives, including fireworks and safety cartridges. You may need a licence or some other permit - contact your inspector for advice.

Some substances, like organic peroxides and other oxidisers, can behave just like explosives if they aren't stored and handled properly. Check labels and hazard data sheets.

See: GN:CS 3, 17;
HS(R) 17, 22

Road Traffic (Carriage of Explosives) Regulations 1989

16 DANGEROUS SUBSTANCES

Some substances used at work are obviously dangerous - concentrated sulphuric acid, for example. But many sub-stances used at work are not obviously hazardous and they sometimes appear unexpectedly.

Hazards may be biological, chemical or physical, and include fire and explosion. Think about the way in which materials are used and whether anyone would be at risk if anything should go wrong. An incorrect decision could lead to immediate injury or long-term illness.

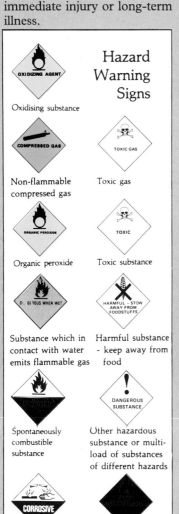

Hazard Warning Signs

Oxidising substance

Non-flammable compressed gas

Toxic gas

Organic peroxide

Toxic

Toxic substance

Substance which in contact with water emits flammable gas

Harmful substance - keep away from food

Spontaneously combustible substance

Other hazardous substance or multi-load of substances of different hazards

Corrosive substance

Flammable liquid

Flammable solid

Flammable gas

The references on these pages are described more fully in the publications list at the back of the book.

BEFORE BUYING

- get the supplier's hazard data sheet (keep a file of these sheets) and explanations from the supplier if necessary

- assess the risk from use or storage - if possible find a safer substitute

- design safe work methods and storage arrangements

- choose protective equipment and clothing

- provide training and instruction

- arrange for any medical checks or health surveillance needed

- draw up emergency procedures.

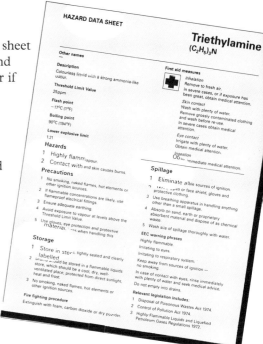

WHEN DANGEROUS SUBSTANCES ARRIVE ON SITE

- give a copy of the hazard data sheet to anyone handling the substance
- display a warning placard, especially if the data sheet is complicated or difficult to understand
- check container labels and consignment notes to make sure that goods supplied are as ordered
- check that handling and storage arrangements are in accordance with the supplier's warning labels and instructions
- provide any special precautions, includ-ing trained supervision for emergencies during unloading or use
- make sure first aid and fire-fighting equipment is readily available at point of use
- display hazard warning signs at the entrance to your premises or at the store.

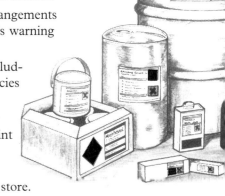

IF YOU ARE A SUPPLIER

- provide hazard data sheets and other information for users

- if manufacturing or importing a new substance see 'SPECIAL CASES' section opposite

- arrange for any necessary testing and research so that substances can be used safely at work

- choose packaging which provides protection for users and during conveyance

- design labels to give adequate information about the risks and necessary precautions (Classification, Packaging and Labelling of Dangerous Substances Regulations 1984 (CPL Regulations))

STORAGE

Certain chemicals may be incompatible in that they can react together to form unstable or noxious products, or can produce heat - which creates a fire risk. Classes of material must be stored correctly in relation to each other; oxidising substances, for example, should be separated from flammable liquids or other flammable substances.

Use information from the supplier and the package label to decide storage arrangements. Materials can be separated by distance, by a physical barrier or (sometimes) by other non-reactive materials which can provide segregation without wasting space.

A safe storage system will:

- separate process areas (where fire or leakage is more likely to occur) from storage areas

- provide specific conditions of storage necessary, such as isolation or separation distances

- prevent incompatible chemicals being mixed eg by spillage, damage to packaging or by wetting during fire fighting

- reduce risk of physical damage eg by fork-lift truck

- prevent rapid spread of fire or smoke, or liquid or molten substances

- minimise the amount of hazardous material involved in any incident

SPECIAL CASES

- if you use or store certain listed ('major hazard') dangerous substances you may need to notify HSE, and demonstrate to your inspector that you are operating safely

- if, as a manufacturer or importer, you are supplying a new substance (ie a substance not on the EINECS list), you should contact HSE for advice on notification   See HS(R)14(Rev)

WATER DISPOSAL

The discharge of effluent, disposal and transport of waste, and the emission of smoke and chemicals to the atmosphere, may need special precautions or authorisation. Contact your inspector or local authority for advice. Contaminated clothing or containers also need careful disposal.

TRANSPORT

- label packages for road conveyance (CPL Regulations) or as required for rail, air or sea transport

- train vehicle drivers in emergency procedures

- check compatibility of vehicle loads (Road Traffic (Carriage of Dangerous Substances in Packages etc) Regulations 1986)

- fit hazard markings on delivery vehicles as required (Dangerous Substances (Conveyance by Road in Road Tankers and Tank Containers) Regulations 1981)

CONSIDER WHAT

COULD GO WRONG

- would smoking, eating or drinking at the workplace increase a health risk?

- could soiled protective clothing or equipment contaminate clean clothing?

- could emergency water supplies freeze up in winter?

- is your supplier's emergency phone number (day and night) readily available?

- could staff inadvertently mix incompatible chemicals - bleach with other cleaners, for instance?

- are you prepared for a large leak or spillage?

- what about hazardous by-products or intermediates?

- could mixing of waste chemicals in the drains cause a hazardous reaction or pollution?

- has any hazardous waste been buried or otherwise contaminated land or buildings?

- if maintenance workers suspected the presence of dangerous substances like asbestos or lead paint, could you handle the problem

GUIDES TO THE LAW

Classification, Packaging and Labelling of Dangerous Substances Regulations 1984 (CPL Regulations)
See: HS(R)22

Dangerous Substances (Conveyance by Road in Road Tankers and Tank Containers) Regulations 1981
See: HS(R)13

Road Traffic (Carriage of Dangerous Substances in Packages etc) Regulations 1986
See: HS(R)24

17 TRANSPORT AND HANDLING MATERIALS

Over 100 people each year die in accidents caused by transport at work. Lifting and moving loads manually is one of the biggest causes of industrial injury. Use these checklists to improve your handling of materials and vehicles.

TRANSPORT

If you operate any vehicles or if vehicles visit your workplace:

- make someone in your firm responsible for transport safety

- have your drivers properly trained and do not allow unauthorised people to drive

- make sure visiting drivers are aware of your rules

- check vehicles daily and have faults rectified promptly

- keep keys secure when vehicles are not in use

- properly supervise vehicle movements - particularly when reversing and near blind corners - using recognised signals

- keep roadways properly maintained and adequately lit

- separate vehicles and pedestrians where practicable. Mark safe crossing places for pedestrians and warn drivers if they are near a footpath

- load and sheet vehicles in a safe place without obstructing traffic. Check that loads are stable and secure

- if passengers are allowed to ride on vehicles, make sure they can do so safely

- protect drivers against falling objects or vehicle roll-over (by tractor safety cabs, for instance).

See: GN:GS 9, 26; HS(G) 6, 19; Safe moves posters 4, 5; AS 16, 22; GN:PM 69; COP 26; Department of Transport Code of Practice - *Safety of loads on vehicles*

DURING VEHICLE REPAIR

make sure brakes are applied and wheels chocked

- always prop raised bodies

- start and run engines with brakes on and in neutral gear

- support vehicles on both jacks and axle stands (never rely on hydraulic jacks alone)

- beware of the explosion risk when draining and repairing fuel tanks, and from battery gases

- use a tyre cage when inflating tyres, particularly with split rim wheels

- avoid burns from battery short circuits

- don't breathe in asbestos dust from brake and clutch linings and pads.

See: AS 16; GN:PM 37, 38; SHW 428

The refrences on these pages are described more fully in the publications list at the back of the book.

SAFE LIFTING

- keep the test certificate for all lifting machinery and tackle showing its safe working load, and the annual or six-monthly examination reports
- use only certified lifting equipment (marked with its safe working load) which is not overdue for examination
- never exceed the safe working load of machines or tackle. Remember that the load in the legs of a sling increases as the angle between the legs increases
- do not lift a load if you doubt its weight or the adequacy of the equipment
- before lifting an unbalanced load find out its centre of gravity. Raise it slightly off the ground and pause - there will be little harm if it drops
- never use makeshift, damaged or badly worn equipment - chains shortened with knots, kinked or twisted wire ropes, frayed or rotted fibre ropes
- provide suitable packing to protect slings from damage by sharp edges of loads and do not allow tackle to be damaged by being dropped or dragged from under a load
- take care to avoid snatch or sudden loads, particularly in cold weather
- cranes should have the correct counterweight, load radius indicator and/or automatic safe load indicator. Have a responsible slinger or banksman and use a recognised signalling system
- make sure that people or loads can't fall from a high level when using lifting machines like lifts, hoists or cranes
- have properly interlocked or key-controlled access to motor rooms and service pits of hoists and lifts

See GN:PM 26, 46, 55

SAFE STACKING

DO ... chock objects which may roll, such as drums, and keep heavy articles near floor level

- inspect pallets, containers and racks regularly for damage. Prevent damage from fork-lift trucks and other vehicles
- stack palletised goods vertically on a level floor so they won't overbalance
- 'key' stacked packages of uniform size like a brick wall so no tier is independent of another
- use a properly constructed rack where possible - and secure it to a wall or floor.

DO NOT ... allow items to protrude from stacks or bins into gangways

- climb racks to reach upper shelves - use a ladder or steps

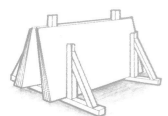

- lean heavy stacks against structural walls
- de-stack by throwing down from the top or pulling out from the bottom
- exceed the safe loading of racks, shelves or floors.

See: GN:PM 15

MANUAL HANDLING

Organise the work to minimise the amount of lifting necessary, using mechanical means or other aids. When help is needed for lifting heavy or awkward loads, get everyone to work together but make sure only one person gives clear, unhurried instructions. Provide protection for hands and feet, and protective clothing where necessary.

Make sure that everyone knows the correct lifting techniques:

- don't jerk and shove -twisting the body may cause injury
- lift in easy stages - floor to knee then from knee to carrying position. Reverse this lifting method when setting the load down.
- hold weights close to the body. Lift with the legs and keep the back straight
- grip loads with palms, not fingertips. Don't change your grip while carrying
- don't let the load obstruct your view. Make sure the route is clear before you start moving.

Many jobs around your workplace may be done using ladders, trestles or scaffolds. These are a major cause of serious accidents, many of which are fatal. Follow these rules to make work at heights safer - and check the safety of contractors working for you.

The references on these pages are described more fully in the publications list at the back of the book.

MOBILE SCAFFOLDS

- refer to the supplier's instruction sheet to calculate the maximum height in relation to the base dimension (including outriggers, if fitted). The base:height ratio is often 1:3
- mobile scaffolds used outside in windy weather should be tied to the building and be anchored or have the base extended by fitting outriggers
- guardrails and toeboards are necessary all round
- provide safe means of access to the working platform - never climb the outside of the tower
- use only on ground which is firm and level
- the working platform should be clear of people and materials when the scaffold is being moved. Move it only by pulling or pushing at the base
- wheels should be fixed to the scaffold, turned outwards to provide maximum base dimensions and wheel brakes must be 'on' and locked when the scaffold is used
- do not overload the working platform or apply pressure which could tilt the tower
- tie the tower to the building before leaving it unattended.

See: GN:GS 42

LADDERS

- secure ladders against slipping by tying at the top. Alternatively secure at the sides or at the foot. A second person standing at the foot to prevent slipping is effective only with ladders less than about 6 m long
- ladders should extend at least 1m above the landing place or the highest rung in use, unless there is a suitable handhold to provide equivalent support
- arrange ways of carrying tools and materials up and down so that both hands are free to grip the ladder
- use a ladder stay or similar device to avoid placing ladders against a fragile surface eg plastic gutters

- never place ladders where there is danger from moving vehicles, overhead cranes or electricity lines
- make sure ladders have level and firm footings - never unsteady bases such as oil drums, boxes or planks. Do not support ladders on their rungs
- extending ladders should have an overlap of at least three rungs
- set ladders at the most stable angel - a slope of four units up to each one out from the base
- check ladders regularly for defects. Never use damaged or 'home-made' ladders. Take them out of use and destroy or repair them.

Follow similar rules with stepladders and trestles.

See: GN:GS 25, 31; IND(S)4(L)

SCAFFOLD SAFETY

How a scaffold is used will determine how substantial it needs to be. Scaffolds should only be designed, erected, altered or dismantled under the direction of a competent person and by competent and experienced workers. Scaffolds should be inspected weekly by a competent person.

Does your scaffold meet the requirements? Check these points as a guide:

1 adequate foundation - placed on level, firm ground with baseplates and soleplates where necessary

2 platform 3-5 boards wide, depending on use

3 each scaffold board on a working platform with at least three supports - supports not more than 1.5 m apart

4 scaffold boards either tied down or overhanging each end support by at least 50 mm and not more than 150 mm

5 vertical supports not more than 2-2.5 m apart

6 scaffold braced along the diagonals to stiffen it both along and at right angles to its length

7 scaffold tied to the building at least every 4 m vertically and 6 m horizontally

8 guardrails and toeboards along the outside edge and at the ends of any working platform from which people or materials could fall more than 2 m

9 toeboards at least 150 mm high with no more than 750 mm between the top of the toeboard and the guardrail

10 guardrail 1 m above the platform

See: GN:GS 15

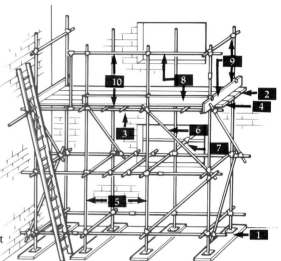

ROOFWORK

More than 20 people die every year at work when they fall off or through roofs. If you, your employees or contractors repair, replace or clean flat or sloping roofs, or need to go on them to inspect them or to get to plant, follow these rules:

- make sure everyone is aware of the precautions to be followed when working at heights - as well as the detailed training of their own job

- fix a prominent permanent warning notice at the approach to any fragile roof

- never walk on fragile materials such as asbestos cement or glass (beware - glass may have been painted over)

- on fragile roofs never walk along the valley gutters, roof ridges or purlins (ie the line of the roof bolts) unless there is something to prevent you falling straight through the roof if you stumble

- on fragile or pitched roofs use suitable crawling boards. Never use less than two boards if you have to move along the roof. Cover fragile skylights on otherwise solid roofs

- even on a flat roof make sure that the edge is protected by a parapet and/or guardrails and that the roof is strong enough to support you

- where someone could fall over the edge of the roof, temporary guardrails and toeboards must be installed or anchorage points for safety belts provided. Make sure that safety belts are worn

- prevent items falling onto people below - use barriers, warning notices or a 'look out'

- unless absolutely necessary don't go onto roofs in bad weather eg high wind (especially if carrying sheet materials) or where there may be other hazards eg fumes from flue outlets.

See: Deadly Maintenance: *Roofs: A study of fatal accidents at work;* HS(G)33

OTHER WORK ABOVE

THE GROUND

- do not use a fork-lift truck as a high level working platform unless it is fitted with a proper cage secured to the forks to prevent falls and access to the chains. The truck should be controlled from within the cage

- fence the edges of platforms which are more than 1.5-2 m above ground with 1 m-high guardrails. Mid-rails, or, for example, brick guards, may also be needed. Do the same around pits and vats

- cover floor openings or put a fence around them

- provide staircases with substantial hand rails if there are more than three risers on a flight, and mark the step edges

- wear safety belts or harnesses when window cleaning or during tree climbing or pruning

- fit safety hoops or rest stages on long vertical fixed ladders used regularly. Fall arrester devices may also be useful

- get experienced and competent persons to install small lifting appliances (eg gin wheels) or boatswain's chairs. They need secure anchorage and an adequate counterweight.

See: GN:PM 28, 30; GN:GS 25; HS(G)19; IND(S)4(L)

19 MAINTENANCE WORK

All businesses are at some time affected by maintenance work - repairing or cleaning machines, plant, vehicles or buildings. Over 100 people are killed each year during maintenance activities at work.

See: Deadly Maintenance: *A study of fatal accidents at work.*

The references on these pages are described more fully in the publications list at the back of the book.

WHAT NEEDS MAINTENANCE?

Buildings, equipment and plant should, for safety's sake, all be maintained in good working order and in good repair. As well as planned maintenance some items are required by law to be regularly checked. Make sure that each of the following is adequately dealt with:

Regular inspections and checks - for example:

> daily inspections of guards by machine operators
> quarterly checks of portable electrical apparatus

Routine lubrication, service and overhaul - for example:

> weekly engine oil top-up
> annual service of fire extinguishers

Legally required inspections or examinations carried out by specially appointed, trained and responsible people - for example:

> inspection of power press guards each shift
> weekly inspection of scaffolds
> monthly examination of rescue equipment

Periodic tests and examination carried out by a 'competent person' (often your insurance company engineer) - for example:

chains and ropes	every 6 months
lifts and hoists	every 6 months
cranes	every 14 months
steam boilers	every 14 months
air receivers	every 26 months

Be guided by the manufacturer's recommendations when working out your own maintenance schedules for items such as vehicles, fork-lift trucks, ventilation plant, ladders, portable electrical equipment, protective clothing and equipment, and machine guards. Check the legal requirements, especially for examinations by a competent person.

BUILDING WORKS

Most activities involving structural work are subject to the Construction Regulations, which specify standards for a wide range of matters, such as safe access and lifting safety. The Regulations apply to construction, structural alteration, repair, maintenance, repointing, redecorating and external cleaning, demolition, site preparation and laying of foundations.

If building works are expected to last six weeks or more you must notify your inspector. Even if you use a contractor you still have legal responsibility for many matters on your premises.

Remember - children are fascinated by ladders, scaffolds and holes in the ground. Don't put them at risk - keep them and all unauthorised people out.

Further information - essentially for firms in the construction industry -

See: GN:GS 7, 25, 28; GN:PM 27, 63; GN:EH 7; GN:CS 6; SS 1-16

DEADLY MAINTENANCE - CASE STUDY

A fitter went into a hopper at a concrete batching plant to repair it. The plant was in continual use and as sand was discharged from the hopper into a mixing vehicle the man was sucked down, buried by sand and asphyxiated. There was no permit to work system and the plant had not been isolated.

Over 350 people have died in the last five years through not taking the proper precautions before entering confined spaces, sludge pits, vats and vessels. Many of them were working alone.

PERMITS TO WORK

During maintenance work, conditions are very different from those normally encountered and new hazards may be introduced. It is essential that everyone concerned is aware of the hazards and of the correct precautions. You may need a written 'permit to work' system for jobs which involve risk of serious personal injury, for example:

- entry into vessels, confined spaces or machines
- hot work which may cause explosion or fire
- construction work or employment of contractors
- cutting into pipework carrying hazardous substances
- mechanical or electrical work requiring isolation of power or fuel supplies
- work on roofs or in excavations
- work on plant, mixers, boilers etc which must be effectively cut off from the possible entry of fumes, gas, liquids or steam.

Special precautions may be needed, for example:

- testing for dangerous fumes or lack of oxygen before entering an unventilated pit or silo
- locking off electrical isolators and dumping hydraulic fluid before starting work inside large machines
- vacuuming the inside of an empty grain silo - to remove dust which might explode - before hot cutting a hole in the side.

When the risk is high, your precautions must be 100% correct. If in doubt, discuss them with your inspector.
See: GN:GS 5

DEMOLITION AND EXCAVATION

Get specialist advice when you intend to dig deeper than one metre. Trench sides may collapse suddenly whatever the nature of the soil. Any excavation deeper than 1.2 m must have the sides sloped or adequately shored.

Keep a clear area around excavations to prevent people, materials or vehicles falling in, and the weight of soil or equipment from causing the sides to collapse.

Beware of poisonous or asphyxiating gases from sewer openings and marshy ground or from pump motors, flammable gases or vapours in confined spaces.

Keep well away from overhead electricity lines and underground services, including cables and gas pipes.

Knocking down walls or other structures requires specialist skills.
See: GN:GS 29

HAND TOOLS

Hammers - avoid split, broken or loose shafts, and worn or chipped heads. Heads must be properly secured to the shafts.

Files - should have a proper handle. Never use them as levers.

Chisels - the cutting edge should be sharpened to the correct angle. Do not allow the head to spread to a mushroom shape - grind off the sides regularly.

Screwdrivers - must never be used as 'chisels' and hammers should never be used on them. Split handles are dangerous.

Spanners - avoid splayed jaws. Scrap any which show signs of slipping. Have enough spanners of the right sizes. Do not improvise by using packing material and extension handles.

ISOLATION

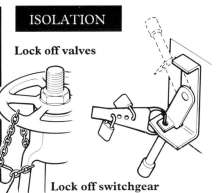

Lock off valves

Lock off switchgear

Before any maintenance, cleaning or adjustment, isolate machines from the main power supply. It is not enough to switch the machine off - the main isolator, usually a separate control, should also be used.

If the machine is at some distance from the isolator, or if work in progress is not readily apparent, remove the fuses from the isolator box and attach a 'danger tag' to it. Better still, after removing the fuses, lock the isolator box (by key direct or padlock) and keep the key safe. Multi-lock and multi-hasp devices can also be used, for example to isolate valves.

WATCH OUT FOR

ASBESTOS

Asbestos is used widely as lagging on plant and pipework, in insulation products such as 'fireproofing' panels and in asbestos-cement roofing sheets. If it is damaged:

- avoid breathing in the dust
- do not work on insulation or sprayed coatings unless you are licensed by HSE
- if you cannot avoid disturbing it, follow the working methods described in the Approved Code of Practice or required by regulations
- well sealed, undamaged asbestos is often best left alone. Make sure all asbestos is clearly identified, sealed and protected against further damage.

See: GN:EH 35, 36, 37, 47

REFERENCE SECTION

1 KNOW THE LAW

*HSE 16	Don't wait until an inspector calls ....: the law on health and safety at work: essential facts for small businesses and the self-employed
*IND(G)1	Articles and substances used at work. The legal duties of designers, manufacturers, importers and suppliers erectors and installers
*IND(G) 97(L)	COSHH and section 6 of the Health and Safety at Work Act.
Poster	Health and safety law, what you should know ISBN 0 11 701424 9
L1	Guide to the HSW Act ISBN 0 11 885555 7

2 GETTING ORGANISED

*IND(G) 2(L)	Mind how you go!
*IND(G) 73(L)	Working alone in safety
*IND(G) 83(L)	Working hours including changes introduced by the Employment Act 1989
*IND(S) 15(L)	Health and safety in small clothing factories
HS(G) 55	Health and safety in kitchens and food preparation areas ISBN 0 11 885427 5

3 SAFE SYSTEMS

†GN:GS 5	Entry into confined spaces ISBN 0 11 883067 8
†GN:GS 30	Health and safety hazards associated with pig husbandry ISBN 0 11 883580 7
†GN:GS 35	Safe custody and handling of bulls on farms and similar premises ISBN 0 11 883515 7

L5 (Rev)	Control of substances hazardous to health, and control of carcinogenic substances - approved code of practice ISBN 0 11 885593 X
*HSC 2	HSW Act: the Act outlined
*HSC 3	HSW Act: advice to employers
*HSC 5	HSW Act: advice to employees
*HSC 6	Writing a safety policy statement: advice to employers
*HSC 7	Regulations, approved codes of practice and guidance literature
*HSC 8	Safety committees: guidance to employers whose employees are not members of recognised independent trade unions

*IAC L1	Guidance on the implementation of safety policies for the construction industry
Booklet	Writing you health and safety policy statement: how to prepare a safety policy statement for a small business ISBN 0 11 885510 7
Booklet	COSHH assessments (a step by step guide to assessment and the skills needed for it). ISBN 0 11 885470 4

*IND(G) 76(L)	Safe systems of work
*IND(S) 27(L)	Safe pressure systems
Booklet	Health and safety for small firms in the print industry ISBN 0 11 883851 2
Booklet	Agricultural black spot - a study of fatal accidents ISBN 0 11 883874 1

REFERENCE SECTION

4 PROTECTIVE CLOTHING AND EQUIPMENT

*HH 2	Construction health hazard information sheet No.2: cold weather	*AI 1	Personal buoyancy equipment on inland and inshore waters	*IND(G) 80(L)	Head protection regulations and you	
				*IND(G) 81(L)	Construction: wear your hard hat	

5 ACCIDENTS AND EMERGENCIES

*IND(G) 3(L)	First aid provision in small workplaces: your questions answered	*HSE 21	Report that accident: RIDDOR the Reporting of Injuries, Diseases and Dangerous Occurrences Regulations 1985	HS(R)23	Guide to Reporting of Injuries, Diseases and Dangerous Occurrences Regulations 1985 ISBN 0 11 883858 X
*HSE 11	Reporting an injury or a dangerous occurrence				
*HSE 17	Reporting a case of disease	HS(R)11	First aid at work ISBN 0 11 883446 0	COP 42	First aid at work ISBN 0 11 885536 0

6 GENERAL WORKING ENVIRONMENT

HS(G)38	Lighting at work ISBN 0 11 883964 0	Booklet	Watch your step: Prevention of tripping, slipping and falling accidents at work ISBN 0 11 883782 6	*IND(G) 69(L)	Violence to staff
HS(G)57	Seating at work ISBN 0 11 885431 3				

7 HEALTH PROBLEMS

*MS(A)1	Lead and you	*IND(G) 57(L)	Review your occupational health needs: Employer's guide ISBN 0 11 883993 4	*IND(G) 84(L)	Leptospirosis. Are you at risk?
*MS(A)7	Cadmium and you			*IND(G) 91(L)	Drug abuse at work. A guide to employers
*MS(B)3	Anthrax	*IND(G) 59(L)	Mental health at work ISBN 0 11 883998 5	*IAC(L)27	Legionnaire's Disease
*MS(B)7	Poisoning by pesticides - first aid	*IND(G) 61(L)	Working with health problems: advice to employers on health aspects of placement and rehabilitation	*IAC(L)28	Precautions against humidifier fever in the print industry
*HSE 5	An introduction to the Employment Medical Advisory Service			*AI 2	Zoonoses in agriculture
†GN:EH 23	Anthrax: health hazards ISBN 0 11 883194 1	*IND(G) 62(L)	Protecting your health at work	HS(G)60	Work related upper limb disorders: a guide to prevention ISBN 0 11 885565 4
†GN:EH 26	Occupational skin diseases: health and safety precautions ISBN 0 11 883374 X	*IND(G) 64(L)	Introducing assessment (COSHH Regulations)		
		*IND(G) 65(L)	Introducing COSHH (Control of Substances Hazardous to Health Regulations 1988)	SHW 355	Dermatitis from flour, dough or sugar ISBN 0 11 883082 1
OP 1	The problem drinker at work ISBN 0 11 883428 2	*IND(G) 67(L)	Hazard and risk explained (COSHH Regulations)	COP 2	Control of lead at work (in support of SI 1980 No 1248) ISBN 0 11 883780 X
*IND(G) 36(L)	Working with VDUs				

8 SAFE USE OF CHEMICALS

*MS(B)6 (Rev)	Save your skin: occupational contact dermatitis	SHW 397	Effects of mineral oil on the skin (cautionary notice) ISBN 0 11 883086 4	Booklet	How to use hair preparations safely in the salon ISBN 0 7176 0263 X
SHW 366	Dermatitis from synthetic resins (cautionary notice) ISBN 0 11 880854 0	COP	Pesticides: Code of Practice for the safe use of pesticides on farms and holdings ISBN 0 11 242892 4	Booklet	A guide to health and safety in GRP fabrication ISBN 0 7176 0294 X
SHW 367	Dermatitis ISBN 0 11 880849 4				

REFERENCE SECTION

9 THE AIR WE BREATHE

*IND(G) 17(L) Asbestos and you

*IND(G) 54(L) Asbestos: does your company work with asbestos?

*IND(G) 63(L) Passive smoking at work

GN:MS 13 (Rev) Asbestos
ISBN 0 11 885402 X

†GN:EH 1 Cadmium: health and safety precautions
ISBN 0 11 883930 6

†GN:EH 2 Chromium: health and safety precautions
ISBN 0 11 883028 7

†GN:EH 5 Trichloroethylene: health and safety precautions
ISBN 0 11 883606 4

†GN:EH 10 (Rev) Asbestos: exposure limits and measurement of air-borne dust concentrations
ISBN 0 11 885552 2

†GN:EH 16 Isocyanates: toxic hazards and precautions
ISBN 0 11 883581 5

†GN:EH 22 Ventilation of the workplace
ISBN 0 11 885403 8

GN:EH 35 (Rev) Probable asbestos dust concentrations at construction processes
ISBN 0 11 885421 6

GN:EH 36 (Rev) Work with asbestos cement
ISBN 0 11 885422 4

GN:EH 37 (Rev) Work with asbestos insulating board
ISBN 0 11 885423 2

GN:EH 40 Occupational exposure limits (updated annually)
ISBN 0 11 885580 8

GN:EH 41 Respiratory protective equipment for use against asbestos
ISBN 0 11 883512 2

GN:EH 42 (Rev) Monitoring strategies for toxic substances
ISBN 0 11 885412 7

†GN:EH 44 Dust in the workplace: general principles of protection
ISBN 0 11 883598 X

†GN:EH 46 Exposure to mineral wools
ISBN 0 11 883521 1

GN:EH 55 The control of exposure to fume from welding, brazing and similar processes
ISBN 0 11 885439 9

HS(R)19 (Rev) Guide to the Asbestos (Licensing) Regulations 1983
ISBN 0 11 885489 5

COP 3 Approved Code of Practice: Work with asbestos insulation, asbestos coating and asbestos insulating board
ISBN 0 11 883979 9

COP 21 Control of Asbestos at Work Regulations 1987
ISBN 0 11 883984 5

†HS(G)37 Introduction to local exhaust ventilation
ISBN 0 11 883954 3

HS(G)53 Respiratory protective equipment: a practical guide for users
ISBN 0 11 885522 0

*MS(B)8 Your health and ...2-pack spray paints

Booklet Respiratory protective equipment; legislative requirements and lists of HSE approved standards and type approved equipment
ISBN 0 11 885428 3

10 NOISE AND VIBRATION

*IAC(L)17 It's your hearing: protect it! Noise alert for construction workers

*IAC(L)21 Noise from portable breakers (construction)

GN:PM 31 Chain saws
ISBN 0 11 883547 5

GN:PM 56 Noise from pneumatic systems
ISBN 0 11 883529 7

Booklet 100 practical applications of noise reduction methods
ISBN 0 11 883691 9

*IND(G) 75(L) Introducing the Noise at Work Regulations

*IND(G) 99(L) Noise at work - leaflet for employees

L3 1-2 Booklets: Noise at work
ISBN 0 11 885512 3
3-8 ISBN 0 11 885430 5

11 RADIATIONS

*IND(S) 9(L) Wear your film badge

†GN:GS 18 Commercial ultra-violet tanning equipment
ISBN 0 11 883553 X

GN:PM 19 Use of lasers for display purposes
ISBN 0 11 883370 7

GN:PM 51 Safety in the use of radio-frequency dielectric heating equipment
ISBN 0 11 883615 3

IAC (Rev) Printing Industry Guidance: Safety in the use of inks, varnishes and lacquers cured by ultra-violet light
ISBN 0 11 885506 9

COP 16 Approved Code of Practice: Protection of persons against ionising radiation arising from any work activity: the Ionising Radiations Regulations 1985
ISBN 0 11 883838 5

COP 23 Exposure to radon the Ionising Radiations Regulations 1985
ISBN 0 11 883978 0

12 ELECTRICITY

*AS 17	Electricity on the farm	
*IND(G) 89(L)	Guidance for small businesses on electricity at work	
GN:GS 24	Electricity on construction sites ISBN 0 11 883570 X	
GN:GS 27	Protection against electric shock ISBN 0 11 883583 1	
GN:GS 37	Flexible leads, plugs, sockets etc ISBN 0 11 883519 X	
GN:GS 38 (Rev)	Electrical test equipment for use by electricians ISBN 0 11 883533 5	

GN:PM 29 (Rev)	Electrical hazards from steam/water pressure cleaners etc ISBN 0 11 883538 6
GN:PM 32	The safe use of portable electrical apparatus ISBN 0 11 883563 7
GN:PM 37	Electrical installations in motor vehicle repair premises ISBN 0 11 883569 6
GN:PM 38	Selection and use of electric hand lamps ISBN 0 11 883582 3
GN:PM 64	Electrical safety in arc welding ISBN 0 11 883938 1

OP 5	Electrostatic ignition: hazards of insulation materials ISBN 0 11 883629 3
HS(G)13	Electrical testing: safety in electrical testing ISBN 0 11 883253 0
HS(G)22	Electrical apparatus for use in potentially explosive atmospheres ISBN 0 11 883746 X
HS(G)38	Lighting at work ISBN 0 11 883964 0
HS(R)25	Memorandum of guidance on the Electricity at Work Regulations 1989 ISBN 0 11 883963 2

13 MACHINERY SAFETY

*AS 11	Circular saws
*AS 20	Safety with chain saws
*AS 24	Power take-off and power take-off shafts
*IND(G) 1(L)(Rev)	Articles and substances used at work; the legal duties of designers, manufacturers, importers and suppliers, and erectors and installers

GN:PM 21	Safety in the use of woodworking machines ISBN 0 11 883380 4
GN:PM 31	Chain saws ISBN 0 11 883547 5
GN:PM 66	Scrap baling machines ISBN 0 11 883936 5
HS(G)17	Safety in the use of abrasive wheels ISBN 0 11 883739 7
HS(G)31	Pie and tart machines ISBN 0 11 883891 1

HS(G)44	Drilling machines: guarding of spindles and attachments ISBN 0 11 885466 6
HS(G)45	Safety in meat preparation: guidance for butchers ISBN 0 11 885461 5
HS(G)55	Health and safety in kitchens and food preparation areas ISBN 0 11 885427 5
L4	Woodworking Machines Regulations 1974: guidance on regulations ISBN 0 11 885592 1

14 FIRE

*HSE 8	Fires and explosions due to the misuse of oxygen
GN:CS 3	Storage and use of sodium chlorate and other similar strong oxidants ISBN 0 11 883523 8
†GN:CS 4	Keeping of LPG in cylinders and similar containers ISBN 0 11 883539 4
†GN:CS 6	The storage and use of LPG on construction sites ISBN 0 11 883391 X
†GN:CS 8	Small scale storage and display of LPG at retail premises ISBN 0 11 883614 5

†GN:CS 15	Cleaning and gas freeing of tanks containing flammable residues ISBN 0 11 883518 1
GN:CS 17	Storage of packaged dangerous substances ISBN 0 11 883526 2
†GN:EH 7	Petroleum based adhesives in building operations ISBN 0 11 883032 5
GN:EH 9	Spraying of highly flammable liquids ISBN 0 11 883034 1
†GN:GS 3	Fire risk in the storage and industrial use of cellular plastics ISBN 0 11 883042 2
†HS(G)1	Safe use and storage of flexible polyurethane foam ISBN 0 11 883208 5

†HS(G)3	Highly flammable materials on construction sites ISBN 0 11 883218 2
†HS(G)4	Highly flammable liquids in the paint industry ISBN 0 11 883219 0
HS(G)5	Hot work: welding and cutting on plant containing flammable materials ISBN 0 11 883229 8
HS(G) 50	Storage of flammable liquids in fixed tanks (up to 10 000 cubic metres) total capacity ISBN 0 11 885532 8
Booklets	General Fire Precautions: Home Office Booklets. *Guide to the Fire Precautions Act 1971.*

REFERENCE SECTION

15 EXPLOSION

*IND(G) 29(L) Introducing competent persons

*IND(G) 35(L) Hot work on tanks and drums

GN:CS 3 Storage and use of sodium chlorate and other similar strong oxidants
ISBN 0 11 883523 8

GN:GS 4 Safety in pressure testing
ISBN 0 11 883043 0

GN:PM 4 High temperature dyeing machines
ISBN 0 11 883049 X

GN:PM 5 (Rev) Automatically controlled steam and hot water boilers
ISBN 0 11 885425 9

GN:PM 22 Training advice on the mounting of abrasive wheels
ISBN 0 11 883558 8

GN:PM 60 Steam boiler blowdown systems
ISBN 0 11 883949 7

HS(G)16 Evaporating and other ovens
ISBN 0 11 883433 9

IIS(G)17 Safety in the use of abrasive wheels
ISBN 0 11 883739 7

HS(G)29 Locomotive boilers
ISBN 0 11 883879 2

HS(G)39 Compressed air safety
ISBN 0 11 885529 8

HS(G)62 Health and safety in tyre and exhaust fitting premises
ISBN 0 11 885594 8

HS(R)17 Guide to the Classification and Labelling of Explosives Regulations 1983
ISBN 0 11 883706 0

HS(R)22 Guide to the Classification, Packaging and Labelling of Dangerous Substances Regulations 1984
ISBN 0 11 883794 X

HS(R)30 A guide to the Pressure Systems and Transportable Gas Containers Regulations
ISBN 0 11 885516 6

COP 37 Safety of pressure systems: pressure systems and transportable gas containers regulations 1989
ISBN 0 11 885514 X

COP 38 Safety of transportable gas containers
ISBN 0 11 885515 8

SHW 428 Inflation of tyres and removal of wheels
ISBN 0 11 880856 7

SHW 830 Dust explosions in factories
ISBN 0 11 880848 6

SHW 849 Nitrate salt baths
ISBN 0 11 880858 3

16 DANGEROUS SUBSTANCES

*AS 27 Pesticides

*IND(G) 93(L) Solvents and you

HS(G)51 Storage of flammable liquids in containers
ISBN 0 11 885533 6

†HS(G)27 (Rev) Substances for use at work: the provision of information
ISBN 0 11 885458 5

HS(R)13 Guide to the Dangerous Substances (Conveyance by Road in Road Tankers and Tank Containers) Regulations 1981
ISBN 0 11 883621 8

HS(R)14 (Rev) Guide to the Notification of New Substances Regulations
ISBN 0 11 885454 2

HS(R)22 Guide to the Classification, Packaging and Labelling of Dangerous Substances Regulations 1984
ISBN 0 11 883794 X

HS(R)24 Guide to the Road Traffic (Carriage of Dangerous Substances in Packages etc) Regulations 1986
ISBN 0 11 883899 7

†GN:CS 19 Storage of approved pesticides: guidance for farmers and other professional users
ISBN 0 11 885406 2

Booklet Guidelines for the safe storage and handling of non-dyestuff chemicals in textile finishing
ISBN 0 11 883833 4

Booklet Chemicals in paper and board mills
ISBN 0 11 883873 3

17 TRANSPORT AND HANDLING MATERIALS

*AS 16 (Rev) Checking tractor-trailer brakes for safety

*AS 22 (Rev) Prevention of tractors overturning

*IND(G) 22(L) Danger! Transport at work (factories)

*IND(G) 78(L) Transport of LPG cylinders by road

*IND(G) 96(L) Are you involved in the transport of dangerous substances by road?

Booklet Safe working with small dumpers
ISBN 0 11 883693 5

GN:GS 9 Road transport in factories
ISBN 0 11 883182 8

GN:GS 26 Access to road tankers
ISBN 0 11 883566 1

GN:GS 39 Training of crane drivers and slingers
ISBN 0 11 883932 2

GN:PM 15	Safety in the use of timber pallets ISBN 0 11 883186 0	GN:PM 46	Wedge and socket anchorages for wire ropes ISBN 0 11 883611 0	HS(G)19	Safety in working with power operated mobile work platforms ISBN 0 11 883628 5

GN:PM 15 — Safety in the use of timber pallets — ISBN 0 11 883186 0
GN:PM 26 — Safety at lift landings — ISBN 0 11 883383 9
GN:PM 37 — Electrical installations in motor vehicle repair premises — ISBN 0 11 883569 6
GN:PM 38 — Selection and use of electric handlamps — ISBN 0 11 883582 3

GN:PM 46 — Wedge and socket anchorages for wire ropes — ISBN 0 11 883611 0
GN:PM 55 — Safe working with overhead travelling cranes — ISBN 0 11 883524 6
GN:PM 69 — Safety in the use of freight containers — ISBN 0 11 883944 6
HS(G)6 — Safety in working with lift trucks — ISBN 0 11 883284 0

HS(G)19 — Safety in working with power operated mobile work platforms — ISBN 0 11 883628 5
SHW 428 — Inflation of tyres and removal of wheels — ISBN 0 11 880856 7
COP — (Department of Transport) Safety of loads on vehicles — ISBN 0 11 550666 7
COP 26 — Rider operated lift trucks: operator training — ISBN 0 11 885459 3

18 PREVENTING FALLS

*IND(S) 4(L) — Preventing falls to window cleaners
GN:GS 15 — General access scaffolds — ISBN 0 11 883545 9
GN:GS 19 — General fire precautions aboard ships being fitted out or under repair — ISBN 0 11 883554 8
GN:GS 25 — Prevention of falls to window cleaners — ISBN 0 11 883573 4

GN:GS 31 — Safe use of ladders, step ladders and trestles — ISBN 0 11 883594 7
GN:GS 42 — Tower scaffolds — ISBN 0 11 883941 1
GN:PM 28 — Working platforms on fork lift trucks — ISBN 0 11 883392 8
GN:PM 30 — Suspended access equipment — ISBN 0 11 883577 7

HS(G)19 — Safety in working with power operated mobile work platforms — ISBN 0 11 883628 5
HS(G)33 — Safety in roofwork — ISBN 0 11 883922 5
Booklet — Deadly Maintenance: Roofs: a study of fatal accidents at work — ISBN 0 11 883804 0
SS 1-16 — Construction safety summary sheets

19 MAINTENANCE WORK

†GN:CS 6 — Storage and use of LPG on construction sites — ISBN 0 11 883391 X
†GN:GS 5 — Entry into confined spaces — ISBN 0 11 883067 8
GN:GS 7 (Rev) — Accidents to children on construction sites — ISBN 0 11 885416 X
GN:GS 25 — Prevention of falls to window cleaners — ISBN 0 11 883573 4
GN:GS 28 — Safe erection of structures (in four parts)
Part 1: — Initial planning and design — ISBN 0 11 883584 X
Part 2: — Site management and procedures — ISBN 0 11 883605 6
Part 3: — Working places and access — ISBN 0 11 883530 0
Part 4: — Legislation and training — ISBN 0 11 883531 9

GN:GS 29 (Rev) — Health and safety in demolition work (in four parts)
Part 1: — Preparation and planning — ISBN 0 11 885405 4
Part 2: — Legislation — ISBN 0 11 883589 0
Part 3: — Techniques — ISBN 0 11 883609 9
Part 4: — Health hazards — ISBN 0 11 883604 8
GN:PM 27 — Construction hoists — ISBN 0 11 883394 4
GN:PM 63 — Inclined hoists used in building and construction work — ISBN 0 11 883945 4
†GN:EH 7 — Petroleum based adhesives in building operations — ISBN 0 11 883032 5
GN:EH 35 (Rev) — Probable asbestos dust concentrations at construction processes — ISBN 0 11 885421 6

GN:EH 36 (Rev) — Work with asbestos cement — ISBN 0 11 885422 4
GN:EH 37 (Rev) — Work with asbestos insulating board — ISBN 0 11 885423 2
GN:EH 47 (Rev) — Provision, use and maintenance of hygiene facilities for work with asbestos insulation and coatings — ISBN 0 11 885567 0
*IND(G) 55(P) — Bitume boilers in construction - fire hazards
*IND(G) 56(P) — Flammable liquids on construction sites
Booklet — Deadly Maintenance: a study of fatal accidents at work — ISBN 0 11 883806 7
Booklet — Fatal Accidents — ISBN 011 885551 4

REFERENCE SECTION

HOW TO OBTAIN PUBLICATIONS

Free publications

For literature and information about HSE free publications contact one of the HSE public enquiry points between 10am and 3pm Monday to Friday:

HSE
Baynards House
1 Chepstow Place
Westbourne Grove
London
W2 4TF
Tel: 071 221 0870

HSE
Broad Lane
Sheffield
S3 7HQ
Tel: 0742 752539

Priced publications

Most priced HSE publications are available from HMSO (see back cover). More specialist publications can be obtained from HSEs sales point at St Hugh's House, Stanley Precinct, Bootle, Merseyside L20 3QY

OTHER SOURCES OF INFORMATION

British Safety Council
National Safety Centre
Chancellors Road
London
W6 9RS
Tel: 071 741 1231

Trades Union Congress
Congress House
Great Russell Street
London
WC1B 3LS
Tel: 071 636 4030

Royal Society for the
Prevention of Accidents
Cannon House
The Priory
Queensway
Birmingham
B4 6BS
Tel: 021 233 2461

Confederation of British Industry
Centre Point
103 New Oxford Street
London
WC1A 1DA
Tel: 071 379 7400

Printed in the United Kingdom for HMSO Dd293856 12/91 C300 3937/2C 12521